I0145837

Taking Applications
Adventures in Internet Dating

by Lyn Noble

A Memoir by
Lyn Noble
Taking Applications-Adventures in Internet Dating
Published by LIQUID Arts & Productions, LLC
Copyright © 2020 by Lyn Noble
Library of Congress

All rights reserved.
No part of this book may be reproduced, distributed, or transmitted in any form by any means, graphic, electronic, or mechanical, including photocopy, recording, taping, or by any information storage or retrieval system, without permission in writing from the publisher, except in the case of reprints in the context of reviews, quotes, or references.
Printed in the United States of America

ISBN: Print: 978-1-7344452-0-6, E-Book: 978-7344452-1-3

Special discounts are available on bulk quantity purchases by book clubs, special interest groups, and associations. For details email: nobledean2313@gmail.com

For information log on to www.noblelove.org

to love

I dedicate this story to all the hope-filled romantics.
Your search may lead you to places you had no idea you'd go
nor that you knew you needed.

*T*his memoir of sorts, *Taking Applications: Adventures in Internet Dating*, was inspired by true events. *When I'd share the details of some of my dates, the listener would say, "You need to write a book!" After hearing that sentiment repeatedly over the years, I set out to do just that—write this book chronicling some of the highlights and lowlights of my Internet dating years and backstory.*

The names of my dates have definitely been changed to protect the guilty... and some innocent folks too! ~ **Lyn**

Contents

Looking for the One
Putting Yourself Out There

"Tis better to have loved and lost than never to have loved at all." ~Alfred Lord Tennyson

I would add the sentiment that once you've experienced what you feel is true love, you long to experience that kind of love again. Ultimately, that was the reason and continued motivation behind my quest or shall I say adventure. I had my one true love, my soul mate, my heart. Life was sweeter than ever. Then he chose another love over me. But I'm getting a little ahead of the story. We'll get back to that. My quest to have "the one" again burned strongly within me.

I've never considered myself desperate to have or get a man. However, I desired to have a male someone special to enhance my life. Family and friends are great to spend time with, but the companionship of a love interest makes life so much sweeter. My passion for life extends to all aspects of who I am whether it's work, family, friends, service to others, theatre, music, etc. Going all out to accomplish whatever is before me has often been the methodological way I operated. My father's voice echoed in my head, "Do it right girl!"

People have described me as friendly, outgoing, loyal,

1

giving, organized, analytical, and a bit of a workaholic. My workaholic tendencies left me to wonder when I would have time to find "the one." Between working more than full-time in a hectic office, going to school, volunteering at church, and hanging out with family and friends (you get the picture) there was no time. Yet, I still yearned at the end of a long day to download, share dinner with someone, give or get a foot massage, be hugged, or have someone other than myself be excited that I was home. The thought of turning into an old lady with eight cats caused me to consider my options for finding a suitable mate. No judgment of those ladies with eight cats, it's just not the plan for me.

~ ~ ~

Where would I find these applicants? The club?

~ ~ ~

As a hiring agent at various points in my career, I've spent many, many hours writing job ads, pouring over applications, and interviewing potential candidates. In the application process the employer is not the only one considering their options. Both the employer and applicant are doing their due diligence to find the right fit. Dating mimics that process. Each party has a set of criteria, sometimes unknown to the other side; nonetheless, the desired qualifications to win the position are essential. One of the most critical steps in the job hiring process was getting and reviewing that initial application. In the interview, you're filling in the blanks and finding out what's not on paper. In essence, you're completing the application. The whole hiring and job search process made sense to apply to my "Search for the One."

Where would I find these applicants? The club? No,

I love to dance but the rest of what goes into being in the club just wasn't my vibe. The bar? Strike that since I really didn't drink. You can't count my once a year birthday strawberry daiquiri as drinking. Especially when I would ask the waitress to make it almost virgin and the drink would still be too strong. Going to the grocery store or a big box home improvement store hoping to meet hunks seemed too ridiculous. The fact that I am totally obsessed with DIY (do it yourself) projects, being in a Home Depot or Lowe's home improvement store for me is like a child on a shopping spree in Toys R Us. I was sure I wouldn't remember that I had gone in to check out cute guys. I'd be too focused on planning out my next home improvement project.

Light bulb moment! Well, that is after receiving numerous spam emails from various Internet sites promising to find my perfect mate. I decided to bite the bullet and give the Internet a try. Besides, where else could I look at and browse through countless seemingly available applicants, oops, I mean, men? Just a note that this was in the infancy of Internet dating, before the Internet became the preferred method of meeting singles, and before swipe left or right was a thing. There was still a certain stigma attached to dating someone you met on the Internet. I felt brave to be making such a bold move. Who knew it would become the norm? Some might even deem it the preferred method.

First, I needed to create a profile. After reading a dozen or so other people's profiles, I got started on mine. Profile contemplated, written, edited, read and re-read, edited again, and pictures attached. Done! Okay, so I'm actually doing this.

Submit! Now just breathe and wait for the responses to come. Jumping into the deep end of the pool when your swimming skills are questionable was a little scary. And so, the adventure began...

Although I think I'm completely adorable, I realized that not everyone was going to like me. I was prepared; rejection is a part of the process. Not everyone is going to be a fit. Chemistry is a real element. You like what you like. Sometimes you just don't gel with that other person. You have to maintain a good attitude and keep it moving. After all, meeting new people is fun! Being up front and polite can go a long way when confronted with the inevitable. Sometimes, you're just not that into him or he's just not that into you. You learn, grow, and keep going.

When I began the process, I thought I'd have a date here or there. I was blessed to meet quite a few nice men. They weren't necessarily for me, nevertheless, they were nice. I didn't realize it would turn into a journey. It was in retrospect that I realized it had become a journey, an adventure. Some of the colorful men who earned nicknames inspired this memoir.

This is probably a good time to stop and explain a few strong elemental characteristics of my personality and background. Generally, I have a sunny, upbeat, and optimistic personality. I definitely have the glass is half full or about to be re-filled attitude. You can often find me laughing or trying to get someone else to laugh. Encouragement is my special power that I use for good. I was raised very old-school by strict parents who expected their thirteen children to tow-the-line. My father had been in the Army and operated with a military mindset. I guess

4   *Taking Applications*

he had to in order to keep things running smoothly. There were rules and we followed them. We always had to address adults as Ma'am or Sir and you only spoke when you were spoken to. These ideals were more standard back in the day (or so I thought); now, not so much.

Being the twelfth of thirteen children, I learned early on to be polite. My mother was always correcting me for saying things very bluntly. She'd say, "You shouldn't just blurt out whatever you're thinking. That's tacky." We weren't even allowed to call our siblings names like dumb, stupid, or liar. We had to say, "You're telling a story" even if they were straight out lying. Foul language was never spoken by my dad or my mom. If my dad used the phrase, "I'll be John Brown…" or my mom said, "Hot dog!" you knew you were in big trouble. That was their versions of losing their tempers and cursing.

I explained all of that because at some point during this book you're going to probably think to yourself, "Why didn't she do this or that?" or "No way I would have done that!" When those thoughts arise, please know that most of the time I was either being extremely polite, a little naive, patient, or considerate of the other person's feelings. Actually, in many situations, I was overly all of those things… to my own detriment.

I hope you enjoy experiencing my adventures.

Taking Applications

Taking Applications

Winky-Blinky

A favorite Twilight Zone episode of mine was the "Will the Real Martian Please Stand Up?" episode where they are trying to determine who the escaped Martian is amongst a group of travelers in a diner. The main character tries to avoid being detected and although he looked like a normal human being during the entire episode, he reveals his true Martian identity to the cook by removing his jacket, which reveals he has a third arm. He announces to the cook that the Martians are now going to take over the earth. The cook laughs as he removes his cap revealing a hidden *third eye* in the middle of his forehead. He laughs diabolically and tells the Martian, "It's too late! I am from Venus. We have intercepted the Martian spacecraft and have already begun colonization of the earth." The episode ends. You just never know about a person, or rather a Martian and Venusian, and what they could be hiding. What, you ask, does that have to do with anything? I'm glad you asked.

I'm having a great conversation with my newest Internet interest. Just getting to know him to determine whether it's worth moving forward with an in-person meeting or not. We shared many of the same basic goals overall. He was active in giving back in both his church and the community. He was very open about his past challenges with alcohol dependency, and to his credit he had been sober for over sixteen years. He was funny, tall, and kind of cute to boot. I jokingly said to him, "What's your third eye?" He got really quiet and had no response. An explanation of The Twilight Zone episode then ensued. He still didn't respond, so I moved on to other topics realizing that he probably didn't like The Twilight Zone show or didn't get my analogy of it in relation to our conversation.

We decided we did want to meet in person and agreed to a dinner date. After a little more conversation, we chose to meet at this cool 24-hour spot in Marina del Rey, Jerry's Deli. It's casual with a huge variety of menu items and a nice ambiance. Prior to our date, we talked on the phone one or two more times but there was no more talk of The Twilight Zone or any possible third eye.

On date night, I did my best impersonation of a "grown, halfway cute, I'm going on a date" woman. I hid my nervousness since this guy seemed to be a good candidate on paper for "the one." I was hoping and praying that he looked like his profile pictures and that he was actually 6'2" as he claimed to be. Being 5'10" in flats made this an important issue for me.

Ah, there he is. Tall, looks like his picture… cool! We gave each other a warm embrace and as we parted he winked at me. I blushed a little and thought, He likes what he sees. He took my hand. We entered the restaurant and were immediately seated. I was a little disappointed that he chose to sit across from me rather than next to me but… well, let me not get ahead of myself. Winky-Blinky sat down, smiled at me and winked again. Now I'm blushing 'cause he must be feeling me. I smiled back and immediately looked down at the enormously large menu the waitress handed me. As I perused the menu and discussed the choices with my flirtatious male companion, he winked at me each time I looked up at him. I thought to myself, He's trying to get the 'cookie' tonight. I smiled back thinking, That's not happening on my watch… well, not tonight!

~ ~ ~

I flashed back in my mind to our conversations. Twilight Zone! This is his "third eye!"

~ ~ ~

We continued to get to know each other and he continued to wink at me. Each time he winked, I felt shy and looked down. The waitress brought our meals. About two or three bites into the meal when we're both chewing, I looked at him and noticed him wink. This time it was a little different because I didn't look away. Then he winked again, and again, and yet again. There it was again. What's going on? Oh wow! He's not winking at me. His winker, or rather his blinker, is broken! I was remembering the baby dolls of my childhood that would close their eyes when you lay them down and open them when you sat them upright. Sometimes the eyes of the doll would malfunction or break and blink or wink randomly. His winker/blinker was broken.

All of sudden, I flashed back in my mind to our conversations. Twilight Zone! This is his "third eye!" Oh my goodness! I went from being so taken aback with all of his flirting to trying to mask my reaction at his little surprise. If I am nothing at all, I am the ultimate polite girl who never wants to hurt anyone's feelings. For what seemed like the next five to ten minutes, I don't think I knew a thing he said. The distraction of all that blinking at me was mind-boggling. Thoughts bounced around in my brain. Gee, no wonder he got quiet when I asked what his third eye was. He probably thought I knew something. He was probably self-conscious and thought I wouldn't go out with him. Should I ask about the blinking? Would that be rude? Get over it. This is really distracting. Don't be so shallow; this is not a real issue. And all the while he's winking and blinking away.

~ ~ ~
Nothing could mess up or rather distract me this time. It would be dark...
~ ~ ~

I honestly don't know how I got through the whole meal. I concentrated on what he was saying and worked on the appropriate responses. In spite of the constant internal dialogue in my head, admittedly, I had a nice time. But could I date him? Could I get past the distraction? Well, maybe I could if I knew more about the what, why, when, etc. I decided I was NOT shallow and should try to handle it. We parted with another hug. He expressed that he had a great time and would like to see me again. I agreed and promised to call him when I got home safely.

Sounds like the end of the story with him, right? Nope. Remember I said I'm polite and NOT shallow. Now I had to prove these things to myself regardless of how distracting the broken

Winker Blinker was. Next time, we chose the trendy Johnnie's Pastrami Restaurant with the fire-pit on the patio. I love a good pastrami! Especially this place; they knew how to do a pastrami sandwich right. Nothing could mess up or rather distract me this time. It would be dark, and I would be focused on not making a mess with the always juicy, tasty, heaping pastrami sandwich.

I arrived before he did and waited in my car parked in front of the restaurant. He arrived shortly after me. Exhibiting his gentlemanly manners, he opened my door and assisted me out of the car. We embraced and as we parted, there it was… blink… blink… blink! I'm in my head again. It's okay. It's not that bad. I wonder what happened to him? Can that be fixed? Should I ask him about it? Would that be rude? It's going to be dark on the patio if we sit out there. Maybe he doesn't know he does that. Someone has to have told him before. Do I have any facial tics I don't know about? Maybe he had a stroke or something.

"Oh yes. I would like to sit on the patio." Okay, girl, pay attention to what he's saying. Stop with the shallowness of looking at his "winking blinking" eye. We got through the date. But I made a decision that I was indeed shallow because I was not able to ask him about the eye thing and I also knew it was too distracting. While I found him interesting, kind of cute, and sexy, I couldn't stay out of my head which meant I was not completely myself. I was too busy trying not to make him feel self-conscious.

We did stay in contact for a while. I ended up doing some layout and design work for a home-based business he had started.

But he had definitely been designated into the friend zone.

~ ~ ~

Over the years when I think about him, I often wonder what could have developed had I opened up and asked him about his eye. What seems like a very simple and obvious solution now eluded me then. My inquisitive nature has matured enough to realize how to maneuver through sensitive topics and situations tactfully.

You live and you learn... and your communication skills mature.

Taking Applications

Taking Applications

NDM

When you think of the perfect date, you might envision some unique activity like skydiving, a hot air balloon ride, sailing at sunset, or perhaps a romantic getaway with wine and cozy conversation in front of a fireplace. Or you could be like me with very little leisure time and consider simple things like a good movie and dinner to be the perfect first date. Loving movies, I figured you couldn't have all that bad of a time. It gives you a built-in conversation should there be that awkward "I don't know what to talk about" lull during dinner. Hopefully, you get to enjoy a good movie. You can tell a lot about a person by their movie going/watching etiquette, which leads me to NDM. I'll explain his nickname later.

I got home from work and kicked off my shoes. Ahh! Pulled out my laptop. Fired up the dating app. Okay, let's see who sent me flirts today. Flirts were in the earlier days of Internet dating the same as swiping right; a quick way of showing interest. NDM sent me a flirt. He likes me, I thought (in my best Sally Field Academy Award speech voice). Hmm… 5'11, check. Owns his own business, cool. Means he's not afraid of hard work and is dedicated to his vision. Included his income, 200K, okay, good. He brings something to the table. I wonder why he included that piece of info? It was an optional profile item that most people left blank. Seems like he might be bragging a bit. Why advertise that? Not a big deal. I'll engage him in conversation at some point about that. Likes some of the same music. So far, I like. Believes in God... great! I could talk to this guy.

After exchanging a few messages through the dating site, we decided to take it live and talk on the phone. He was articulate, witty, and engaging in his conversation. Like me, he also had a busy work schedule from running his own business. We talked about his business, my job, the challenges of having very little spare time, trying to live a healthier lifestyle, and a few other topics.

He was a big guy. Not football big; more like Sumo wrestler big. This would be my first time dating a big boy. Surprising since I'm a fluffy type myself. His size didn't bother me at all, just more to love. He was on a journey to lose significant weight and had already proudly lost over 90 pounds. I shared his enthusiasm at his accomplishment as I was also on a quest to improve my eating lifestyle and become less fluffy. Side note: I had been calling myself fluffy well before the fantastic comedian Gabriel Iglesias became famous. I love him; he is hilarious! Back to NDM. This would be great! I'd have a partner in the struggle, rather, journey in losing weight.

We found that we also shared a love for the big screen. We talked at length about the latest movie releases and decided that we would meet after I got off work to catch a movie.

I should take pause to say that NDM had already earned two strikes with me, but I wasn't counting. Initially, he had wanted me to drive to a theater very near to his home in the Long Beach area instead of meeting at a midpoint location. At the time I lived in an area north of Los Angeles, in the San Fernando Valley. Meeting in his area would require I fight through 405 freeway traffic. This freeway is known to have some of the worst traffic in the country hands down. I had nicknamed it the moving parking lot. Most folks avoid it at all costs. Meeting at a midpoint would have made the most sense. His insistence that I come to his area in Long Beach was extremely off-putting. I politely eased out of further talk of catching a movie and ended the phone call. Forget the movie with him. I could go to the movies anytime. If he wasn't willing to drive for a first date, what else would he not be willing to compromise on? I had better ways to spend my time.

An hour later, he called back, apologized, and asked would I reconsider going out with him. He didn't know what he had been thinking, he said. I thought about it and said okay. We set a date, time, and theater where we'd meet. It wasn't in his area. Strangely, a midway point now seemed like a good idea to him.

The day of the date arrived. The phone rang. NDM was on the line. We exchanged small talk then he pops off the question, "Is it okay with you if we go Dutch?" I was silent. My brain began to process his line of thinking. First of all, I am not Dutch, don't know nothin' bout going Dutch on a date, and definitely not a first date. Isn't he supposed to be trying to impress me? Especially when he thought it necessary to state he made two hundred thousand US dollars a year? I was NOT impressed. Instead of speaking my mind, I sarcastically agreed and decided to ignore the stupidity of his cheapness. Besides, I was curious and the little birdie kept telling me to stop being so picky. I've since killed off that little birdie! (No actual birds were killed during my adventures in Internet dating)

After pulling a full shift at work with no breaks or lunch, I freshened up a bit and dashed out of work to meet NDM at the movie theater. We arrived at practically the same time and immediately sized each other up. He was cute with a capital C! And yes, he was a big guy, very nicely dressed, and he smelled yummy. He smiled at me and suggested we go inside.

~ ~ ~
"What should we do next?" he asked. "Have some dinner at P.F. Chang's would be nice!!! I yelled...
~ ~ ~

With his go Dutch policy in the forefront of my mind, I suggested he pick up the tickets and I'd get the movie snacks. He agreed. He then told me he didn't want popcorn because of his strict diet. He was proud to remind me of his 90 pounds lost to date. I understood and let him know I hadn't eaten all day and was definitely going to have popcorn... with butter and salt. Besides, who can resist popcorn at the movies? He decided on water only.

We settled in our seats, chatted, and I munched on the

popcorn until the previews came on. A little while into the movie, I was still enjoying the popcorn and offered my date some expecting him to decline. I was just being polite. He accepted and took the bucket from me. Time passed and he didn't give it back. Hmm! He sure is enjoying my popcorn. I thought to myself, I thought he didn't want any popcorn… especially not with butter and salt. That's okay. He's probably hungry. Turns out he was very hungry. He ate the rest of the popcorn without offering me a kernel. Wow! This guy.

It was a good movie and I was looking forward to discussing it over dinner. There was a P.F. Chang's directly across the courtyard from the theater. I could already taste the shrimp with candied walnuts and melon served over steamed rice. As we walked out of the theater doors, I headed for the restaurant. When I got to the door, I waited for NDM to open it but he hesitated. "I'm not hungry," he volunteers. I reply, "Well, I need to get something to eat, I haven't eaten all day. Maybe you could have a salad or something." Of course he's not hungry, he just ate the rest of my popcorn, I thought. He walked away from the restaurant and headed toward the benches in the courtyard. "It's after six and I can't eat anything else." I was still standing by the door in astonishment wondering where he was going.

Resigned, I followed and joined him on the bench. He proceeded to say what a wonderful evening it was and how much he had enjoyed the movie. And then, "What should we do next?" he asked. Have some dinner at P.F. Chang's would be nice!!! I yelled inside my head. "I worked right through lunch today. I could eat and you could watch," I said jokingly. The lecture then ensued about his strict diet and his weight loss journey. He went on to say that he doesn't eat after a certain time no matter what. It was clear that there was no dinner happening, hence his nickname, No Dinner Man (NDM). So, I dropped the subject and began to think of a way to end this date politely. I was done with him. I was hangry before that term had become a thing. While I contemplated my dilemma, NDM started a conversation with a patrolling security guard who was making his rounds. The guard was a little on the hefty side but nothing like my sumo wrestler-sized date. When I focused into the dialogue, NDM was giving the security guard weight loss advice that bordered on a lecture. As best as I could tell, the information he was giving was not solicited nor welcomed. I was embarrassed for all of us. No one wants weight loss advice from someone bigger than them. It was uncomfortable and unnecessary. I had to do something quick.

"Well, I better get going," I interrupted. "I'm parked in the other lot. Can you walk me to my car?" I asked. He replied, "I can't walk that far. I'll give you a ride." He explained he had bad knees and was parked in the handicap area very near to where we were seated. Cautiously, I followed him to his very nice, tricked out Escalade. I was breaking one of my rules by getting in his car but thought he couldn't be all that bad if he drove such a nice car, even if he was inconsiderate and cheap when it came to my needs, especially dinner. Besides, I could definitely outrun him [sheepish smile].

He drove me to my car. I thanked him. For what, I don't know. That politeness thing was in full effect. He launched into full conversation saying he didn't want the date to end yet and couldn't we talk some more. My suspicion proved correct that he actually just wanted to make out, as the kids say. After a few minutes of futile conversation, I managed to extricate myself from his car without being mauled too much. Finally, end of date!

I've heard a popular talk show host say that a man will ghost you instead of providing closure to a woman. The man doesn't want to deal with confrontation; he'd rather just disappear without explanation. I had decided that I was definitely going to go typical male and ghost NDM. That night was going to be the last he would ever see or hear of me.

I was so wrong. He called numerous times expressing interest in getting together again. Gathering up my courage and forthrightness, I confessed exactly why I did not want to go out with him anymore. After reminding him of his no dinner antics, he came to his own defense by saying we had not made plans for dinner. If I had wanted dinner, I should have made that clear before making plans to see the movie, he argued. Trying to reason with him about such a simple, common sense issue seemed to be an exercise in futility. Besides, I could buy my own dinner! In spite of numerous invitations to go out with him again (even a dinner invite), I did not accept.

It's funny that I didn't have to change his name for the retelling of this portion of my adventure because I don't remember it. He will forever be known in my mind as No Dinner Man.

And then there was the sequel.

Taking Applications

Memah's Gourmet Coffee Shoppe

NDM Too

Taking Applications

NDM Too

You do like coffee, right? No full chapter for this guy that I nicknamed NDM Too, just an un-honorable mention for his lameness.

I had a few unspoken rules, like if I'm going to get dolled up and make the effort to go out with you, then we need to do something basic. I'm not talking about anything extravagant. Again, more like a movie, dinner, a walk on the beach, and good conversation. Mr. NDM Too, however, needed to get his coffee on. I don't like coffee. I actually love the way it smells but not the taste. Although I own a Keurig and will occasionally hit up that famous coffee place, it would usually be to get a hibiscus iced tea with one of my coffee loving friends.

Just coffee, no meal, translated to me as cheap or lazy; the guy just wants to see what I look like with minimal effort. I understood this strategy, but I didn't like it. Then why did I agree to coffee? I was trying something new, trying to step outside of my box, and trying to be flexible.

I could tell immediately that NDM Too wasn't feeling me from the moment he saw me. He didn't even try to hide his displeasure. I wasn't impressed with him either. There was zero chemistry on either side. My posted pictures were a true reflection of my actual self. The photos were recently taken in various scenarios including full body shots. I have never understood why people post outdated photos or just head shots on their profiles. Eventually, you're going to meet in person, and they will see the truth. Although my profile was upfront and accurate, his was not. He did not look like his picture and was shorter than he had listed. Maybe he had used Photoshop. Bummer.

We ordered drinks anyway; coffee for him and tea for me. We sat on the patio trying to get through a conversation. It was one of the lamest dating experiences during my journey. I didn't really blame him for trying to end the date early, but the excuse he finally gave was pitiful. I actually felt a little sorry for him. I could have let him off the hook and ended the date myself, but I didn't. In retrospect, it may have been because I felt a certain way about the whole coffee shop thing.

So, explain away he did. He explained in unnecessary detail that his mother's floors were very dirty. He had promised to buy her a new mop and give her floors a good cleaning that evening. He even talked about the kind of mop he needed to buy because she had a Swiffer, which was not going to get the job done. It was why he had suggested only meeting for coffee. "And as a matter of fact, I should get going." "Oh, okay," I replied, as I concealed my eye roll. "No problem," I said. I wanted out of there as badly as he did. He barely walked me back to my car. It was comical because halfway to my car he veered off towards his own and said bye as he drifted farther away. I watched him walk really fast to his car. I thought he was going to break into a full sprint. I guess I just wasn't his cup of coffee. It did not make me sad.

That was my last coffee shop date.

Taking Applications

Sexy Man

As with most adventures, they do not always turn out the way you expect. The twists and turns, ups and downs, and surprises both good and bad kept things interesting, exciting, funny, and sometimes frightening.

At first, I thought any site would do for my search. My strategy to use different web sites seemed like a good idea. After a while, I decided that the Christian sites would have better options. I figured the Christian guys had a leg up on the men from the other sites because they were men of faith. We would have basic beliefs in common right off the bat. I would come to know that was not necessarily a true story. The range of beliefs and levels of maturity in their Christian faith ran the full spectrum of what it means to be Christian.

I had long admired a couple of my Christian girl friends that had been holding out for the right guy. Sharing my dating stories with them and getting their feedback gave me a different perspective. My proactive approach to having the right man in my life was completely foreign to their "just patiently wait on God to send the right one" viewpoints. From time to time, that sentiment would color my decisions and cause me to suspend my dating adventures. Mostly, I was encouraged by their input to continue on my trek and work towards keeping true to my goal of celibacy when I felt tempted.

A prime example of one suitor from the Christian site was a guy I'll call Sexy Man. We had several interesting conversations on the phone. Every time I would try to get to know him, he would somehow steer the conversation towards sexual questions. In my opinion, passion and a healthy sense of sexuality are key parts of a great relationship. I was previously married, so I was no prude; however, I did not want sex to be in the forefront of our initial conversations. I also didn't think it was a good idea to tell guys on the first call or two that I was practicing celibacy and that my goal was to wait until I found "the one." Good applicants would get this information only after determining whether I was planning on keeping their application on file or not. Then, they could decide if they were even interested in the job... I mean, me.

On the second or third phone call Sexy Man asked if I received his encouraging text message that he sent earlier in the day; the one with the sunrise and sunset? I had. It was the kind of message that you had to hit the play icon to view. There was an inspirational message on each photo. To my utter shock, I would also find a somewhat hidden photo sandwiched between the sunrise and sunset pictures that flashed very quickly. I had to replay the message twice to verify I had not imagined what I thought I saw. He had included a photo of a "package." When I asked him about it, he proudly asked, "Did you like it?"

I did not. I deleted the text. The realization came at that point that the "package" was his "package." I thought it was totally inappropriate but only said, "That's not cool" in my best Bueller voice. I quickly ended the conversation and decided not to take any more of his calls. He was not a match.

~~~
## Sexy Man just wanted me to know what he was working with
~~~

When I shared this story with one of my brothers, he explained that my overexposed suitor probably thought that I would be impressed. Another male friend joked that Sexy Man just wanted me to know what he was working with. "Wow!" I thought. Really? My friend wanted to know if I was planning on going out with the guy.

The next day, Sexy Man called again. Right off the bat, he began to ask about what kind of sex I liked. I let him know that we could discuss the subject a little further down the road once we got to know each other better. I told him I wasn't comfortable talking in detail about sex so early into the process. He pressed me further, forcing me to drop the big C word on him.

"I'm practicing celibacy," I confessed. I figured he needed to know so that he could take the sex talk down several levels. It took him a few seconds to digest that piece of information, after which he said, "Celibacy? What does that mean? Does that mean that you don't do anything, like even oral or anal or anything?" He could not understand at all. Total disbelief on my part was an understatement. I didn't know what he thought the definition of celibacy was and I really didn't care at that point.

Ironically, I was pulling up to the church for a rehearsal. I took a minute to explain that I was not interested in going any further. We did not view things the same; there was no meeting of the minds. I shook my head as I walked into the church and wondered, "Wow, what was that all about?"

Sexy Man would not be the only man to have me scratching my head in wonder.

I did not go out with him.

Taking Applications

Taking Applications

Triple P

I also met this tall, good-looking, drink of water on a Christian dating site. Triple P was very down to Earth, well-spoken, witty, and easy to talk with. In my mind, it was a bonus that he shared a name with a very famous debonair heartthrob of the silver screen, but he earned the nickname Triple P after our first date.

Our initial phone conversations were pleasant. He was able to clear many of my low hurdles with ease. I didn't want to operate like an interrogator and decided I could find out more meaty information about him if we decided to meet. He loved being by the water and people watching like I did. We decided to go to the Redondo Beach Pier and enjoy the beautiful California weather.

Since he had recently undergone knee surgery, he asked if I wouldn't mind driving and of course picking him up at his place. Actually, I did mind driving and picking him up. "Okay," I said before I could stop myself. We decided on a date and time. He gave me his address. Date planned, we ended the call with mutual expressions of looking forward to meeting in person. The little voice in my head whispered, "You're picking him up?

Seriously?" I quietly replied to the voice, "He had knee surgery. It will be okay."

I parked, assessed my reflection for a last-minute inspection, and patiently waited for Triple P. As he approached the car, I took him in. Tall, cute, dressed nicely, and looked like his profile picture. But why is he wearing sandals and white socks? That was a random thought to pop into my head. I got out of the car and gave him a hug. We cheerfully headed off to the beach.

It turned out to be a picture-perfect, sunny California day. People were out in mass enjoying the pier. We walked, talked, and people watched. Groups of men were fishing at one section of the pier; some had children in tow. Mothers chased their toddlers. Couples of all ages, shapes, and colors walked hand in hand. Teenagers laughed and did what teenagers do when they hang out in groups and no parents are in the mix.

We stood at the railing and looked at the waves breaking and talked some more. We spotted what we decided was a sea lion and imagined what would happen if we fell in. Would it attack us? Were there any sharks in the water? Could we swim to shore? It was a relaxed, pleasant time. He took my hand. I smiled. He pulled me closer to him and came in for a kiss; I returned his advance. It was a sweet, gentle kiss. Nice lips! I thought. What a nice time we were having.

As afternoon turned to evening, we made our way along the boardwalk hand in hand to get a closer listen to the music we heard coming from one of the restaurant bars. It was a simple and romantic date so far with lots of flirting on his part and me blushing as we walked and talked. We moved to the other side of the pier near the rocks where the waves were breaking. This was like one of the hundreds of romance novels I had read. Good live music drifted through the air. The scent of fresh churros and the ocean surrounded us. The night lighting had activated all along the pier. What had been a beautiful day transitioned into a beautiful summer evening.

We sat on a nearby bench in silence looking at the breaking waves. Sometimes silence is golden. Several minutes into the silence, this silly woman wondered what Triple P was thinking. You know… inquiring minds want to know. So, I sweetly said, "You're so quiet. What are you thinking about?" He continued looking at the water and said (rather matter-of-factly), "I want to eat your p_____." He didn't even look at me when he said it. "What?!!!" I exclaimed with my mouth hanging open in utter shock. He repeated, "I want to eat your p_____." My brain was in shock. I closed my mouth while my brain began to shout, Abort date. Abort date. Abooooooorrrt daaaaaaaaaaaatte!!!

P number one!

I drove us there. I would have to get him back home. I reasoned that it was my responsibility to return him. And I planned to return him. My schoolgirl romance novel fantasy date bubble had been popped. Oh boy, hadn't events turned so quickly? Meanwhile, he was still enjoying looking at the gentle waves lapping the rocks. My calm exterior did not mirror the panic and shock inside my head. Various strategies to end the date and get this man home battled in my mind.

"Well, it really is getting late. We should head out. I've got a lot of driving in front of me," I said as calmly and sweetly as I could muster. I could not let him know how I was really feeling. I stood up and started walking towards my car. He followed but wasn't able to get close enough to hold my hand anymore. He caught up in time to open my car door and make sure I was situated before going around to the passenger side. I admit, I thought about just taking off while he was on his way to the other side of the car but the polite girl in me waited. I couldn't leave him stranded with a bum knee and no ride home. Uber had not been invented yet.

On our way back to his place, he asked if we could stop and get a bite to eat. I told him I was really tired and wanted to get home. That was not a true story. I was in fact very hungry. However, his statement about his desires to eat me had completely distracted me from anything else. I was now on a major mission to dump him where I had picked him up. Like, I didn't even know if I'd let the car come to a complete stop when we got there.

He insisted. "We could just go through a drive-thru," he offered. Triple P pointed out a Carl's Jr. in the nearby shopping center. Resigned, I agreed to stop. He ordered. I lied and said I wasn't hungry thinking I could hurry the process along by not eating. In the time between the order board and the pick-up window, he had the gall to ask, "Can you pay? I realized earlier that I forgot my wallet."

P number two!

Wow, I really picked a winner. The old "I forgot my wallet" excuse was in full effect. I paid. Then before I could fully digest that mess, he said, "Let's park and talk." Again, I said, "I'm really tired. Let me get you home." … I parked.

He was still making pleasant conversation as though nothing out of the ordinary was happening. He was clueless to my change in mood. He went right on talking about this and that. I could barely hear him because I just wanted the night to end. He was telling me a story about his ex-girlfriend when he dropped the *"third P"* on me. Well, I guess it was really the *"fourth P"* if we count the whole "Can we park?" P. The girlfriend had cheated on him while he was in the pen… **penitentiary**… blah, blah, blah, blur of words spoken. Penitentiary was where my brain stopped.

Right then, the vision of his sock-sandal combo and my earlier random thoughts came back to mind. In a conversation at some other time that I can't pinpoint, I was told that guys in jail wear socks with their sandals. I can't remember why or any other details. I just retained that random piece of information that popped into my too busy brain once Triple P said penitentiary.

This penitentiary business should have been disclosed to me much earlier in the process. I should have been a better detective and given him the third degree, conducted a Spanish Inquisition, given him shock treatment, put him under bright lights in an interrogation room; all of that and a bag of chips.

My cute, romantic date had transformed in front of my eyes into a man I didn't want to have anything to do with. No thoughts of how he was probably a completely reformed man entered my mind. I did not ask him why he had gone to the pen or why he thought it was okay to say the thing he had said to me. Triple P had been a complete gentleman on the phone and on the entire date. He had been kind-hearted and funny.

He had shocked me and now I was scared of him. I did not tell him that not having his wallet was totally unacceptable to me. I also did not tell him that I wanted to get the heck outta there. But I should have. I would reflect on these things much later. I deposited him back to his place and drove home. There was no goodnight kiss.

The next day, a cheerful Triple P called to say he had enjoyed hanging out with me. After taking a deep breath, I admitted to also enjoying his company. I did until the P's came to light. He wanted to take me out properly very soon. I put my big girl pants on and informed him that I didn't think he and I were on the same wavelength. He tried to offer that we had enjoyed each other, right? I agreed but then asked him if he remembered what he had said to me. He didn't know what I was talking about.

I refreshed his memory of my question to him. "You know, when I asked you what you were thinking?" "Ok yeah," he said. "You know what you said?" I replied. Incredulously, he said, "What did I say? Why are you upset?" In wonder I said, "You said you wanted to eat my p____!" "Oh, that. Well, you're a beautiful woman and you asked me what I was thinking; so,

I told you. That's no reason not to go out with me. You are fine and I want you. (Short pause.) When can I see you again?"

~ ~ ~
My perspective swayed my behavior to the point of acting on my fear
~ ~ ~

I guess I should have been flattered. I was not. He went on to tell me that he had prayed to find a beautiful Christian woman like me. And that when he had kissed me, he knew he wanted to know me more. In spite of all he said, I declined another date. He would continue to call me now and then to see how I was. He would tell me he had been praying and had thought about me; he just wanted to hear my voice. He would ask if I would consider changing my mind.

I was not open to him. I heard him but had made up my mind not to get involved with him. I had decided that a man that did not know better than to blurt out such a crass statement on a first date was not the man for me. How could I trust him to make decisions for me when such a basic thing eluded him? How could I take this unpredictable man into my world? He didn't even understand why his statement had bothered me.

Whether I was being prudish or not was questionable. If he had said that to me in the confines of a committed relationship, my reaction would have been completely different; but, his honest disclosure on a first date made it a game changer. My thoughts were that a man of faith should have speech to reflect that. My diamond in the rough date was most likely a very fine man with a good heart that didn't know any better yet. Nevertheless, I did not wait around to find out. In retrospect, I have no idea why I was so afraid of him. My perspective swayed my behavior to the point of acting on my fear of the unknown and the unspoken. If I had spent more time listening to what he was trying to tell me perhaps I could have been the recipient of something, someone wonderful.

Sometimes someone's past is just that... the past.

Taking Applications

Will? Naw man!
Your name is Paul, right?!
No. It's Will.
Oh, Ok...Paul?
WILL

Taking Applications

Will

Count on the big mouth of my brother-in-law to ruin a moment. I'm visiting my sister Mona with my new guy, Will, whom I had decided was going to be a keeper. He had already been throwing the "M" word around and I was thinking it was a good idea. After all, I wasn't getting any younger. My internal timer told me I'd better get married before I expired. People are always saying age is only a number, blah, blah, blah. My brain wasn't going for that; I was not twenty anymore.

Marc, Mona's husband, came in from work. I greeted him and introduced Will. "Nice to meet you man! What did you say your name is?" "Will... Will?!" Hearty laughter ensues; that belly holding type. He was slapping the counter-top, pointing at me, and laughing hard. Just as I was formulating the question in my mind "What's so funny?" A realization in his face transferred to my brain. Then I saw what was coming. In all of Will and me getting to know each other, I had failed to mention my last three serious relationships had a common factor. A factor that unbeknownst to me, Marc found hilarious. I didn't even think it was a "thing." I had actually forgotten. Really. Marc jumped right in to have some fun at my expense. "Man, I don't know how you got through the screening process? Your middle name is Paul, right? You don't have to lie to me man. She only dates guys named Paul"

There was a common denominator during one period of my life. I can't tell you how many men named Paul I knew. Some of my family and friends seemed to think that I had only dated men named Paul. It seemed like a true story, but it wasn't. It was just a coincidence that three men I cared enough about to bring around the family happened to be named Paul. Thus, "The Paul Years." I'll get back to Will later.

Taking Applications

It's Raining Pauls Hallelujah!

Taking Applications

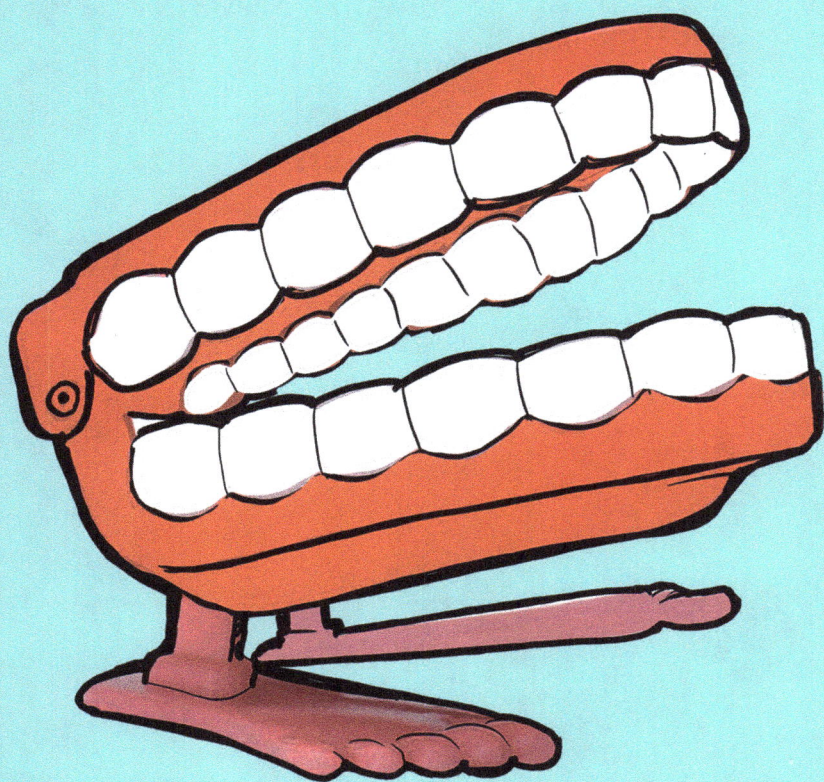

Veggie Paul

Taking Applications

Veggie Paul

Veggie Paul and I were seated in the quaint little breakfast shop. Although Solvang, California, is only two to three hours north of Los Angeles, it was as though we had been transported into another time and place. The cobbled path that led to the restaurant and the frilly little curtains that hung at the windows looked so authentically Danish; it was a totally charming atmosphere. I took in the details of the place while I patiently waited for my companion to choose something, anything to eat.

Being a vegetarian back before it was a popular trend, Paul was having a hard time finding something to suit his dietary requirements and appetite. He finally decided to order a double portion of the steamed vegetables. We engaged in very light banter as we waited and I tried to mask my complete irritation with him. While waiting, I retraced the events of the previous night in my mind.

~ ~ ~

The weekend trip was supposed to be a getaway from all the hustle and bustle of my frantic schedule. He had told me that I worked too hard and deserved a break. He wanted to take me away to just relax and pamper me. He would take care of everything! I believed him. However, up to that point, the trip had been one very frustrating moment mounted upon another very frustrating moment.

We had arrived very late the night before after fighting five hours of horrible traffic because we had left at the peak of "weekend getaway" traffic. We showed up in Solvang on a weekend that also had a huge event that caused all of the hotel rooms to be booked. He hadn't made any reservations. After two hours of driving around trying to find a vacancy, we finally found an open room.

I was so relieved until he began to check-in and didn't have a credit card nor any cash. I was not silent. I discreetly began questioning him. "Why don't you have a credit card? Why didn't you make reservations? How did you think we'd be able to check-in without a credit card or money? This is NOT relaxing," I said. He had not taken care of everything. He then explained that he had planned to get cash once we got to Solvang. "What?!!!" I exclaimed. The hotel clerk caught the expression on my face, quickly assessed the situation, and offered to hold the room.

I was livid but held my cool. Making a scene is not what I do. I thanked her and exited the lobby. Our adventure (not in a good way) continued with us looking for an ATM in the tiny, little town. This was before you could gain access to cash everywhere; there was no Maps app to find the nearest ATM. Most places had already closed for the night. We eventually found money, returned to the hotel, and checked in. By the time we got to the room, I was completely over the moon with anger.

I'm not the type to scream and holler when angry. I was eerily quiet until he tried to hug me. "Don't - you - touch - me! Don't even talk to me. I'm going to sleep!" I told him with utter disgust and then readied myself for bed.

~ ~ ~

The waitress returned with our orders, interrupting my mental trip down memory lane of the previous night's events. Our food looked fantastic and I was ready to eat. Paul blessed the food and began to dig in. I tasted my dish and looked up just in time to see my vegetarian friend's teeth fall into his plate. Okay, let me explain. No, I did not know he had false teeth until that shocking moment.

Although I was reliving my previous night's anger moments before this, I was completely polite and did not want him to feel embarrassed. I turned away and pretended to search for something in my purse to allow him time to put his pride, rather, his teeth back in his mouth. Instead of popping them back in, Paul began to mumble his disgust that his vegetables weren't soft enough and that they hadn't steamed them long enough, etc.

Meanwhile, I continued to rummage around in my purse looking for the imaginary item until he could get himself together. After what seemed like a full minute, he replaced his dentures. He didn't explain anything; he didn't make any comment at all. I took my face out of my purse and attempted to act like all things were normal. Nothing was normal. Nothing was ever normal after that weekend. It's a hilariously funny memory now, then it was just surprisingly shocking.

Internet dating is not how I had met Veggie Paul; however,

my experience with him led me to an amazing love. I met Veggie Paul through an applied music program at El Camino College I had auditioned for and was chosen to participate in. The program required me to login five hours of mandatory practice per week on campus. I was to dutifully hone my vocal skills in the practice room.

One particular Saturday morning, I wasn't so into my vocal studies and decided to take a bathroom break. While returning to my practice room, I heard some wonderful jazz music coming from an unknown location. My musically nosy self had to find its origin. After a little game of "you're getting warmer, no you're getting colder," I found a few cats around the corner in a room with the door opened playing a popular Van Morrison tune. I stood outside trying to be discreet and remain undetected. They sounded pretty good. In my nosiness, I stole a closer listen; one of the guys noticed me standing there and invited me in. "Hey, aren't you in applied music on Wednesday nights?" He asked. "Yes," I replied.

Before I knew it, they had talked me into jamming with them. A little vocal scatting and a few piano chords later, we were all fast friends. From time to time I would see them and sit in on piano for a bit. Once, their bassist started talking to me about his love for ministry and mentoring young men in his church. At the time, I was married, so I wasn't interested in him at all. I thought it was admirable that he was focused on music, had a heart for God, and was serving Him.

Years later, my oldest son would express interest in playing the bass guitar. I thought back to Veggie Paul's mention of tutoring bass and mentoring youth. I dug through my old school contacts and found his card. We figured out the particulars of a tutoring agreement and set an appointment for the first lesson. Side note: By this time, my marriage was no more; however, I still wasn't looking for anything. My hands were full with work, my two sons, and life.

My son's first lesson went well and we made plans to continue with more lessons. I offered to give Veggie Paul a ride home when I found out he had to take the bus back home and it was a bit of a trek. He had done a favor for me by giving me such a reasonable rate, so I wanted to return the kind deed. On our way to his house, we had a really interesting conversation about ministry and I started getting a case of the feels. You know, like I feel like this is a really good conversation and he feels like a really nice, sweet guy type of thing.

A few lessons into the process, my teenage son lost interest in taking bass lessons and moved on to his next thing. Veggie Paul and I had formed a friendship that quickly turned into a romantic thing. It was short-lived because it just wasn't a fit for either of us. After about six months, I realized going to church with him and to some of his casual gigs was not enough for the relationship to last. He was kind but not as on top of his life and things in general.

My thoughts of ending the relationship were cemented with our weekend getaway fiasco. Shortly after our weekend, I politely ended things. Funny thing is he didn't seem to care when I informed him we should part ways. He just said okay.

As an uncomplicated woman, of course I took his

nonchalant reaction in stride. Nope! My feelings were hurt that he didn't seem to care that I was quitting him. He didn't even try to change my mind. After all of the shared meals, rehearsals, Sundays spent ministering together, going to the blues jams at the cool little coffee shop, and hanging out every other Sunday, he just said, "Okay" as though it didn't faze him one way or another. It didn't take me long to get over the dejected feelings because I knew he just wasn't the right person for me.

The silver lining...

The silver lining of my relationship with Veggie Paul was meeting Meg. As a result of attending the bi-monthly blues gigs with him I met Meg, the blues band's manager. She would have a regular group of musicians grooving the blues as other interested singers and musicians signed up to get their turn on stage. It was an open mic type of situation with the house band still making up the majority of performers on stage at any given time. I'd sit and chitchat with her during the jams and we formed a friendship. After Veggie Paul and I parted ways, I kept in touch with Meg from time to time at the blues jams.

No matter what, Veggies are always good for you.

Taking Applications

Paul ~ The Music & Me

Taking Applications

Paul ~ The Music and Me

"**Girl**, what is going on with that hair?" my sister exclaimed. "I know, I know. I'm on my way to see Meg about her girl who's gonna hook me up!" The next day, I met up with Meg at the coffee house. After she gave me her hair braider's info, Meg invited me to sit in and take a listen to the blues band jamming.

The band was doing their thing and sounding good. I asked where Veggie Paul was. He usually sat in on bass. "Haven't been using him," she responded as she pointed to the guy who was playing in his place. I noticed a familiar face. I thought to myself, I know that guy, but from where? Oh, I think that's the guy from my applied music class. I asked Meg. "What's his name?" "Paul," she said. "Paul, that's right. I know him," I explained.

He saw me from the stage and acknowledged me. On his break, he came over and we started talking about school. Paul invited me outside to continue the conversation and to get some fresh air (only to find he really needed a cigarette—the opposite of fresh air—and I was not a smoker). After many apologies about the smoking, how he really needed to give it up, and how he was a bad Christian to be smoking, I told him there was no need to be sorry. "We're all works in progress; God loves us as we are. He'll help you conquer your addiction," I encouraged him. Cough, cough, cough.

And so, a friendship was hatched. We laughed about the old applied music days and reminisced about all the folks we endured week to week who had lots of heart but not so much in the talent department. He complimented me on my singing abilities and commented on how he'd always wanted to collaborate musically. I told him that I thought his little stick bass was the funniest looking bass I'd ever seen. "It's lightweight to gig with," he explained. In spite of his crazy looking bass, his music skills back then were impressive.

He suggested I should come see him play some time in Beverly Hills at this really cool bar and restaurant with a fish tank running through the floor. He would put my name on the list. I thought it was a great idea, so we exchanged numbers. It couldn't have been more than a week or two later when Paul called to say he'd be gigging at that spot on Friday night and did I want to come? My boys were off with their daddy for the weekend, so I said yes.

When I arrived at the up-scaled Crustacean Beverly Hills restaurant, the red ropes were up and the stereotypical big-bodied gatekeeper was checking the list. A quick glance at the list and I was granted entry. Now that was pretty cool. I had never needed to be on a list to gain entry to a restaurant before. As promised, Paul had put me on the list. I liked that.

As soon as I walked through the door, I spotted Paul on the bandstand doing his thing on the upright bass. The band sounded really good. He noticed me right away; his face lit up and he smiled at me. For some reason that I didn't quite understand yet, I felt a flutter in my chest. I thought, "What was that?" I found a seat at the bar, ordered a diet Coke, and began to take in the scene. Just as he had described, there was a fish aquarium running through the entire bar and restaurant floor. I had never seen anything like it. The bar area had a nice vibe with the live music and upscale decor. The Beverly Hills crowd was having a good time.

Please understand that Paul was not my type. He was much shorter than me (okay, two inches was a lot to me) and also not the athletic type. I did not consider this to be a date. I had come with my "support my musician friend" brain. Confusion at his reaction when he saw me and my internal response to it was swirling around in my head. My heart fluttered with excitement. I chalked it up to being free for the night, no kids, and being out on the town.

The music was intoxicatedly good. I was impressed with the band and focused on what Paul was doing on the double bass. On his breaks between sets, he would come over, bring me another diet Coke, and talk. We talked, laughed, and had an easy time. I felt at home with him, as though we had been friends for years. Paul invited me to grab a bite after he was done. Well… it was really getting late, or rather early because they were playing until 2:00 a.m. I was tired but having a good time, so I decided to be that grown woman who was free for the night.

That night (morning), we ended up eating really healthy food, Pink's Hot dogs, and talked till dawn. It was the beginning of the best relationship I'd ever known. From that day forward, we talked nearly every day for three years. Conversation with us was seamless. We had a comfort with each other that made sharing any and everything easy. The discussions had depth, color, and passion. We didn't always agree, but we never argued. We just discussed the topic till we exhausted or tired of it.

Paul had a great ability to listen and retain important pieces of information about me. One such example was the Eartha Kitt incident. We made what I thought was a random trip to the record store, not knowing that Paul had already scoped out the place. This particular Tower Records location had an extensive inventory of rare offerings on both vinyl and CD. Because I was a vinyl collector and loved vintage music, he knew this would be a real treat for me.

I stumbled across a remastered Eartha Kitt CD. It featured a variety of songs. Some were from the 50's, one was in Portuguese and it also included two of my favorite songs by her: "I Want to Be Evil" and "Santa Baby." I was in Heaven as Eartha Kitt was a favorite artist of mine because of the uniqueness of her voice and her smashing of color lines. Paul snapped it up and added it to my collection. We listened to that CD often, enjoying the colors of her voice and the awesome musicians that backed her. Enjoying the same music to the depths that we did was almost spiritual.

About six months later, Paul called me at work. "Hey, Babe, what are you doing on Tuesday the 28th.?" which was about two weeks away. "Nothing, I think." He had me promise to hold the date open. He said, "Don't schedule anything. I've got a surprise for you." I'm hard to surprise so this was going to be an interesting two weeks. "Cool," I told him. As the time neared the date, Paul kept dropping hints trying to get me to guess the surprise. He had said it was something unique that I would particularly enjoy.

"Umm. Would anyone love it?" I asked. "No, but a lot of people with taste would." "Oh, it's something to do with food, right?" "Nope. Guess again," he teased. That went on right up to the point of driving to the venue. We were pulling into the parking lot across from the venue which I now knew was Catalina Bar & Grill. "Do you know where we are now?" he asked. I still had no clue what the surprise could possibly be and why he was so sure I'd like what was coming. I had been there once before but didn't have a clue why we were going there.

As we exited the car and approached the venue, another couple that was leaving the venue and coming towards us said, "Enjoy the show. Eartha was great!" My mouth popped open in astonishment. I looked over at Paul. I exclaimed, "Eartha! Eartha Kitt! We're gonna see Eartha Kitt?!" He was laughing proudly at his success. He had totally surprised me. I was about to see her very up close and personal. The Hollywood venue is a popular intimate jazz club that probably seats no more than one or two hundred people, if that. We had fantastic seats in the second row of tables.

Eartha was amazing! She was in her 70's at the time. Her voice was as strong as ever. She hadn't lost a note. Eartha wore this beautiful form-fitting beaded gown and exuded a classy, sensual vibe the entire show. Ms. Kitt made a young twenty something year old guy in the front row the object of her flirt fest. At one point, she crawled on his table like Cat Woman and sang seductively to him. Yet, the entire show was done with class.

After the show, I was in for another surprise. Paul was friends with Eartha Kitt's bassist. He introduced me to his friend who in turn asked me if I wanted to meet Ms. Kitt. "Do I want to meet her? Oh, yes," I calmly exclaimed, trying not to be that crazed fan. A few minutes later, we were escorted to her private dressing room. As I entered, she approached me and began hugging me. Inside my head, I was repeating Eartha Kitt is hugging me! Eartha - Kitt - is - hugging - meeeee! I managed to speak to her like a normal person and expressed my appreciation for her. She spoke just as I had seen her on numerous occasions on film and television.

She sounded like Cat Woman. Eartha Kitt exhibited total elegance and class. That experience remains my favorite celebrity experience; all because I had this amazing man in my life that really knew me and exhibited ways to bring me joy. We reciprocated this trait with each other.

Our love for music and God would be the basis for an unbelievable love relationship. Never knowing that the very things that bound us together would be the very same things to rip us apart years later. Paul's music always came first; everything else was a distant second, third, and fourth. We would collaborate in music ministry and perform together at a few corporate events. I grew and learned so much from Paul musically. He turned me on to the local jazz scene at the musician's level.

I was meeting and being in the room with the coolest musical cats. Paul played it all and very well, from Broadway to swing, pop, funk, and jazz. His talent was as intoxicating as his laid back, witty, passionate, and gentle personality.

Paul won my heart over and over again. Our late night talks until all hours of the morning; watching him stroke his bass like a well-loved woman; letters written while out to sea where he poured out his heart in poetic prose; kisses so tender it felt like a dream; sharp wit; kindness; and, strength. Those were the characteristics I discovered and fell in love with. He was my gift from God. He understood me. He became my best friend, my confidant, my partner in adventures, and my love. The memory of his love would be the foundation that sparked my desire to try again, to search for "the one."

He wrote me incredible letters throughout our relationship. I'm sharing one such letter written from the middle of the ocean at Christmas time. The letter warmed my lonely, aching heart and I've kept it for when I'm an old lady. He had been out on an extended contract playing bass for the cruise lines.

He wrote (in part):

"My Dearest Darling Lyn,
I hope this letter finds its way to you in time for Christmas; just as I hope I will find my way back to the warmth of your embrace and the sweetness of your kisses when I finally return to you. My soul longs for the day!

I have a few thoughts I would like to share with you. I really care about playing this music as well as I possibly can. I really make it my mission to play very well every night. Lately, before I go on stage, I have felt God Himself telling me, "Relax, I love you, so don't worry."

I feel very grateful to have been blessed with a woman like you who I feel can understand these things. I was thinking this afternoon about how when I was twenty-one years old and had just been saved, I prayed to meet a good Christian woman that loved me and I could love in return. I knew that somewhere she was out there and someday we would meet.

Life can sometimes have a funny way of getting one off course. Everyone gets distracted from time to time. We are still only human. My distractions have included, as you know, three important relationships prior to you. Necessary if only to produce my child, a blessing of course, and to show me what I did not want from a relationship.

So anyway, almost twenty years later, I'm out here in the middle of the ocean just thinking about how much I love you and how glad I am that we have each other. You have everything I have ever really cared about in a woman. You are so beautiful, so bright, funny, and charming. You have so much class and talent. And on top of that, you are very sexy.

I thank God for you. I am grateful that God could make it possible for me to meet and be in love with someone as genuine as you are. I have always felt that you are very honest and real. You don't play games. What you see is what you get. That is a quality that I think is very rare these days; a quality that I have seen you exhibit often, not only to me but to others as well. I hope life never hardens you to a point where you lose that.

I love you for so many reasons. I love your face, your lips, your... I love the way you smile. I think of that smile often out here. It can really warm my soul and help me feel not so lonely even though I can't help but miss you. God knows I miss you so much. It can really hurt, missing you the way I do.

My prayer, the prayer of my heart (God says that if you believe in Him that He will grant you the desires of your heart according to His riches in glory), I think, is that when we are finally able to share our lives again in person, that God sees fit to make our experience together exceed both of our wildest expectations.
Until then, the memory of your sweetness keeps my soul strong and my heart beating time to the song that is you, the sweetest music I have ever heard.

With all my love, Paul

This letter and so many other things made me know that Paul was "the one." Years later, he would tell me that he had not been mature enough, not ready enough to do what was right by me. All of the traveling to distant lands with women offering themselves to him and his inability to not give in to the temptations would cause our undoing. His lonely heart and overactive libido took the easy road that kills so many long-distance relationships.

He had been in and out traveling on contracts for over a year when he came back to the states in between one of his contracts. Paul confessed that he had been unfaithful and ended our relationship. He did not want to be dishonest anymore. His conscious made him come clean, he said. He was deeply apologetic and said he'd understand if I hated him.

I didn't hate him, but I was crushed, stunned, and caught totally off guard. To say that I was hurt would have been a gross understatement. At first, I was so devastated. Days after his revelation, I crumbled; I literally crumbled to the ground on the street at the thought of never having him in my life again. I was distraught and in despair. I was mad at God. I could barely breathe let alone pray. Shamefully, I admit that I tried to destroy my favorite Bible in a fit of rage. I didn't throw it away, but I tore pages out of it and flung them to the floor during my childish tantrum. Later, I would pick it all up through tears and put the pages back in order (much like my life). I would repent for trying to destroy it, for having rage at God, and for putting Paul before God.

The pain experienced during that period was so intense it paralleled the intense love that had built up in my heart for Paul. The pain was on the other end of the pendulum swing. Coming back to the middle was a journey in itself; it would take years. There were so many tears, prayers, times of reflection, trips to the beach for comfort to quiet my mind, and cries out to God for healing.

This was one time in my life when I thought I'd actually die from the emotional pain of our breakup. I thought my heart would never heal enough to love another. I had cried and poured my heart out to my friends and family until even I was tired of hearing my own pain out loud. I felt like I was emotionally throwing up on people. I decided I needed to cope some other way.

My journal became my outlet, my safe place for a combination of crying out to God and venting. I prayed, read my Word, and cried some more while still trying to live a normal life. Time would pass and I would read back over my journal entries. I began to see again that God was there with me all along. He had never left me. I was discovering who I was all over again. As time progressed, a new woman was emerging. I was growing through the pain. Time actually does help to dull the pain; at least it did for me. My faith that God ultimately had me in His arms and loved me was the key to the real healing my heart so desperately needed.

As a young girl, reading was one of my first loves. Romance novels came on the scene for me in my pre-teen and young teen years. Sometimes, I'd escape into the main character's shoes and feel the intensity of the story as if it was my own. When Paul broke my heart, I became the main character in my own story of love lost with no chance of a surprise happy ending. My hero didn't want me anymore because I wasn't enough.

A very sad song became the soundtrack playing in the background of my life as I moved through daily tasks trying to look normal on the outside. Having children did not afford me the luxury to outwardly waddle in my extreme pain. I couldn't fall apart. I had to smile! When the tears would try to take over and pull me into deep depression, I hid myself away in the Word; in my kids; in family; in service to others; in work; and many, many times in music and humor.

My go to best friend and confidant (other than Paul) was my mom. A mother's love has the ability to soothe you like nothing else. We were always able to talk about almost anything. I credited her for some of the healing leaps I made. There is nothing quite like your mama's soothing voice saying, "It's gonna be okay and I love you!" She was always right on time with phone calls and letters. During a particularly difficult time, my mom sent a customized card (I have it to this day) with this encouraging inscription:

"I've been thinking about you a lot lately, and I want you to know how much I care for you—but even more how much God cares for you. I'd love to share with you the incredible love and peace I've discovered—and for you to know that no matter how your circumstances have made you feel, you are genuinely special, eternally valued, and loved without condition." ~Mama

Numerous people in my circle were patiently there for me while the pendulum centered itself. Eventually, pleasant memories began to overshadow the pain and loss. I had loved and lost. I had loved. I had lost. But I knew what love was... in person. Love personified. I had felt something, someone. My heart's dream. My fantasies came true… for a while.

Our relationship had grown to such a beautiful place; it had such rhythm, harmony, and melody. But then Paul had begun to travel for his gigs. I remember the first ship contract he booked was sixteen days. "Sixteen days?!" I asked him incredulously. I thought I would literally die without him for that long. We were absolutely thrilled at the opportunity. Off he went. His dream of traveling with his music career was coming true and he had my full support. I just didn't know how I'd endure him being gone sixteen long days.

The company contracting talent for the ships loved him; he was a hit. They expressed interest while he was still on that trip. Shortly after the first tour, another offer came in for a longer gig, and then another. Before I knew it, they were offering him an international dream contract in Dubai that he couldn't refuse… and he didn't. It became an unwanted long-distance relationship. The cliché was often repeated to me in encouragement, "Absence makes the heart grow fonder. He'll be back before you know it."

We corresponded almost daily whenever he had communication capabilities. There were many international phone calls at all hours of the day and night. Our longing for our continued connection burned strong. We were able to correspond through e-mail often. We tried to download our days and consult one another in email as if we were still face to face. The physical letters like the one I shared earlier were especially cherished communications and endeared him to me even more.

But long-distance is long-distance. Sometimes, not

always, but sometimes no amount of communication can overcome the challenges of being alone in a foreign land, missing everything and everyone yet living your career goals, and having numerous women interested in you as though you were a rock star. It was too much for our relationship.

Paul had spoken to my heart over and over in ways I had only dreamed about before I met him. His level of communication and attentiveness surpassed anything I could have hoped for. Until of course, it became obvious that he had not been communicating honestly with me for a considerable amount of time near the end of the relationship. The music, though muted, still lives on in my heart. Time passed and I healed to the point of wanting to venture out and have my heart sing again.

Melody and rhythm would never be the same...

Taking Applications

Taking Applications

Chuck, Lyn! Lyn!

Many of the men I would meet were nice, intelligent, fun-loving, up-standing people; others, not so much. I don't think that I would have considered the journey an adventure had I not met some of the colorful characters (men) featured. I had some regular "nothing to see here" dates; however, I will never forget some of the others. Just to be clear, I was not always at my best either. I'm sure there are a few guys with stories about me from their vantage point.

Sometimes, I behaved badly. Just that simple. One such example would be my date with Chuck. "Lyn! Lyn!" He called out. "Lyn! Lyn!" He repeated sounding slightly panicked. "Lyyyyyn!" He yelled out again as I angled my walking pattern further away from him. Have you ever decided you didn't want to do something right in the middle of doing that thing?

Note: Rudeness is not an acceptable behavior. Yet, I tried to retreat from my date on first sight. Chuck hadn't seen me exit my car. I saw him first from a distance. The spur of the moment decision was made to act like I hadn't seen him, and furthermore that I wasn't me. I should have just gotten back into the car and drove off. Instead, as he was trying to get my attention, I was being rude and ignoring him... totally! He called out my name over and over. I ignored him.

He sort of had it coming since he hadn't been truthful about his appearance. You cannot lie away several missing inches and post pictures from a long, long, long time ago. His posted pictures (all two of them) must have been taken 10 to 15 years earlier. Old Chuck had not aged well, and we weren't old yet! He had a strange walk and was dressed weirdly. Our planned date was to have lunch on the pier. I didn't know what he was dressed for, but from a distance I had decided that I didn't want any part of him. He wore some pants that looked like something from the 80's not two thousand anything; I think they were corduroy. The shirt was also out of style. I don't remember the color or any other details. I must have blocked it all out or it just wasn't that memorable.

We were to meet south of the pier and walk to the restaurant for lunch. He was determined to get my attention. He was very close to me now. "Lyn!!!" he said with urgency. "Oh, hi," I said sheepishly. Resigned that I could no longer act like I wasn't me, because I looked like my photos, I acknowledged him.

The date happened. People use a term now that totally describes the whole date—meh. Chuck did call me several times asking for a second date without a shred of success. I had zero interest and for once stuck to my guns."That's it for this guy!"~Joe Pesci in the movie My Cousin Vinny

Taking Applications

Three-Piece Suit
and a
Facerag aka Washcloth

Taking Applications

Three-Piece Suit and a Face Rag aka Washcloth

Some applications should have been immediately thrown into the trash. Three Piece Suit and a Face Rag was that application. He was my lesson on safety and listening to your inner voice. They were lessons I already knew but chose to ignore. Sometimes the sounds of life can drown out common sense and the ability to hear those still, small voices trying to guide you.

After several phone conversations about a little bit of everything, Three Piece invited me to enjoy some karaoke. It turned out to be at a bowling alley. This was not a deal-breaker for me; I thought it was quaint. The night arrived. We had agreed to meet at the venue.

My first impression was, "He's a little overdressed." He had on a pinstriped three piece suit and very nice shoes. Stacey Adams, I think. My second and third thoughts were, Well, although we're at a bowling alley, we're not bowling and It's better that he's overdressed than under dressed. He gave me a sweet little hug with a peck on the cheek. I could smell his cologne. Nice, not too much. My senses were appeased with the fact that he was 6'1 as promised and had that ex-football player build, a few extra pounds on top of a linebacker frame.

We were seated and drink orders were taken. A diet coke for me, a rum & coke for him. Hmm, I thought we were both non-drinkers. *Shut uplittle voice. I'm trying to have a date over here.* We had a little chitchat type conversation going. It was fairly benign, nothing really memorable. We listened to several people do their thing with varying degrees of singing abilities. Although I could carry a tune, I had no intention of getting up there, especially not on a first date. Besides, It was more fun to watch.

My handsome date decided he would take a stab at a song or two. 3-Piece was ready to take his turn on the mike after he had polished off a couple of drinks. He approached the staging area, gave me a little wink and then to my surprise dedicated the song to me. I blushed. He was pretty good and sang his second song with equal success. The proud troubadour returned to the table to my supportive applause. We continued to talk a while and then agreed it was getting late. I had thoughts of having something to eat but he didn't offer dinner. However, on our way out, he stopped at the little food stand in the bowling alley and ordered himself something to go. And…no, he did NOT ask me if I wanted anything. He just ordered and then waited for it. If a guy doesn't show regard for you on a first date when he's supposed to be trying to impress you, when will he? My inner voice is now trying to tell me "This dude is a loser." But I just stood there looking a little stupid, if I'm honest. The woman I am today would have ordered what I wanted, told him about himself without making a dramatic scene and kept it moving. After his "to go" order was ready, the date ended with him walking me to my car and giving me a hug. He tried to get a kiss but I was in no mood for affection from him once I realized how inconsiderate he was about the food. I'm not that "scared to eat in front of a man" kind of woman. I'm also not a pig. We parted ways with him saying he'd like to see me again and asked that I call him when I got home safely, which I did.

My forensics of the date made me determine that 3-piece was probably not the guy for me. Later, I would re-visit my first impressions with "Girl, why didn't you listen to yourself?" 3-piece called me the next day to express how much he enjoyed my company and when could he see me again? I told him I had a nice time but was disappointed with the whole food ordering situation and not feeding me. He apologized profusely and said what amounted to a bunch of "blah, blah, blah." He then began to tell me how he could "burn" (slang term meaning to cook really well) when it came to BBQ'ing anything. I listened politely. Eventually, after several more phone calls and boasts of how great his BBQ skills were, he invited me to a home-cooked BBQ dinner. My resolve softened and I decided to let him redeem himself. We made plans to meet at his place for this "wonderful" BBQ dinner and a movie. Note: This was way before there was a Netflix & chill situation.

At this point I should probably explain that I met this man on a Christian dating site. He actually professed to be a practicing Christian, a man of faith looking for a woman of faith.

In a previous conversation, I had disclosed that I was practicing celebacy as a part of my faith walk. He didn't seem to be bothered by the comment and I assumed that we were on the same page. I saw what I wanted to see and had a false sense of security because I thought he was a believer.

I arrived in his neighborhood and drove up and down the street trying to find the location. After my fourth trip down the same street, I called him to ask where the address was located. It was one of those weird addresses with a ½ number in the address. His building was tucked in the back of another house as a rear unit and was nearly impossible to spot at night. He came out to assist me in finding him. I saw a guy standing outside, but this couldn't be my Mr. Three Piece Suit. This guy was wearing a wife beater undershirt and shabby looking jeans. Low and behold, the guy was waving his arms at me, motioning that I had found the place. He didn't come open my door and escort me to his place. Instead, he turned around and started back to his unit. I thought, that's kind of rude, but continued down the path to his place.

There are times when your inner voice does NOT speak quietly. Yet I still managed to ignore it and forge on through the date. I surveyed the tiny studio apartment as I stepped through the door. He took a seat in front of his computer to finish a game he was playing. I looked around to figure out where I could sit thinking, What is going on here? In front of me was a sofa bed that was still in bed form and unmade. I wasn't going to sit there. Why hadn't he cleaned up his place? He had been practically begging me for almost three weeks to come to dinner. This man was a business owner. I thought his place would be better put together even if he was a bachelor. To my left was the tiny kitchen with dishes piled up in the sink and a couple of pots on the stove. There was one very small table and one chair. Maybe I should engage him in conversation about his enthralling game.

Me: "So... what are you playing?"
Him: "World Conquest" (or something)
Me: "What's the object of the game?"
Him: "To conquer the world." (With a side eye look towards me)
Me: "Oh, okay. Well..."
Him: "I'll be done soon. The food's not ready yet."

You're probably asking yourself what was I doing while he was playing? Standing there watching him play the game and thinking, I need to get the heck out of here. This guy is crazy. But no, I just stood there and waited for the next thing to happen. I was trying to make the best of the situation. It was as though I was bothering him, interrupting his quality computer time.

He continued on with his game without regard for his invited guest, finished the game, and then magically remembered I was there. "I've got some wine chilling for you," he offered. I tried a sweet, "No thank you." Since number one, I don't really drink and number two, I definitely didn't drink and drive. Even with the reminder that I didn't drink, he insisted it was really good wine and a little wine with dinner, blah, blah, blah. It wasn't good wine; it was a cheap, screw top, non frou-frou vintage. Resigned, I politely accepted and pretended to sip a bit here and there. He brought the chair from the computer over to the kitchen table and offered me a seat... finally!

Three Piece said the food should be done in a few more minutes but he'd get me started with a salad. To my complete surprise, salad was served in a purple plastic cereal bowl and consisted of sliced cucumbers with bottled Italian dressing. No lettuce, no tomatoes, no croûtons, it was just sliced cucumbers. He didn't join me while I ate my "salad" because he was finishing the BBQ... wait for it... chicken legs. Really? Just chicken legs; no thighs, breasts, or ribs. But I graciously ate what was placed before me.

A few bites into the meal, I asked for a napkin. After much shuffling around in search of said napkin, I informed him that a paper towel would be okay too. He excused himself to the bathroom and you've probably guessed by now, he returned to hand me a washcloth, except he said, "Here's a face rag. I don't have any paper towels." After dinner I was getting the heck outta' there or so I thought. Prior to the finish of dinner, he excused himself again to use the bathroom... with the door open. I could hear him! Remember it was a small studio apartment. Everything was right there.

When we both had finished eating, I began my exit speeches about how it was getting late, of being tired, getting a rain check on the movie, and thank you for dinner. But he wasn't having it. He wanted to watch the movies he had picked out for us. After too much protesting from him, I agreed to stay for one movie. This was a night of surprises. He pulled out his collection of bootleg movies to watch. I pause to say, I am a movie person and enjoy the technical quality of theater quality movies. I realize there's a whole bunch of folks who don't mind watching sub-par bootleg movies. I'm not one of them.

Next issue was where could I sit. He pointed to the sofa bed that was still in bed form. I said no to that. He said, "Oh, it's okay; I'll sit on the floor next to you. It'll be fine. Go ahead, have a seat. I'll put the movie on." With much trepidation, I sat down and he turned the movie on. We watched the movie for about ten minutes when he decided he needed to caress my leg. I removed his hand. He chilled for about two seconds, then started rubbing my thigh again. Before I could react to that move, he got up off the floor, sat next to me, and began kissing me very aggressively. "Hold on! Let's just watch the movie," I suggested.

I can't describe how quickly what seemed like a benign evening turned into his mouth all over me, his hands pulling off my clothes, and him forcing himself into me. The quiet little voice in my head that had been trying to warn me all evening was now in full panic and screaming out loud in my own voice. I pleaded with Three Piece to stop. "Please, no! Don't do this! Please! I really liked you! Stop!"

The voice began to pray out loud to God and Three Piece to spare me. I prayed that this man would have mercy on me and stop what he was doing. I yelled at him, "I am celibate! What are you doing to me? Please! Stop!" I struggled to get him off me. I tried gathering my clothes and running. He caught me, pinned me to the counter, and continued to violate me. My prayers got louder and more fervent. I was crying and praying and begging him to stop. I just kept screaming, "No! Stop! Please!" By the grace of God, he released me. He just stopped and let go.

I was shaken, panicked, and crying. I did my best to pull my clothes on, grab everything, and run out of there. I didn't know why he stopped or why he let me go, but I didn't look back nor question anything. I just ran as quickly as I could back to my car, started the ignition, and drove off. I was so shaken that I crashed into the center median when I turned off his street. I ended up pulling over to the curb and sobbing loudly then softer as I slowed my breathing trying to calm myself. After about ten minutes, I gathered myself and started home.

~ ~ ~

my accusatory yelling voice that screamed out loud, "You're really stupid!"

~ ~ ~

The entire night and all the mistakes I had made played over and over in my head. The quiet voice had been replaced by my very loud self-loathing, accusatory yelling voice that screamed out loud, "You're really stupid!" And it kept reverberating through my mind over and over. I know that I am not stupid but very stupid mistakes were made that night.

Had wanting to find a real connection made me loose focus on safety and common sense? Why had I chosen to ignore the safety rules I had set up for myself? Listening to my inner voice was not even in the equation that night. Instead, voices from folks telling me, "You're too picky" and "Try something different. Get outside of your box," took the foreground. The reality of my rules still should have applied. The rules were in place for a reason. When I chose to ignore them and not listen to the quiet voices, I told myself, "This is what stupid gets!"

I thanked God repeatedly on my drive home, utterly grateful to be alive and relatively unscathed. The forensics of my bad date swirled around my brain. All the missteps and unnecessary chances taken in the quest to connect with someone like-minded could have cost me my life. Optimism and a false sense of trust because I believed he was what he said he was, that he was what I wanted—a man of faith, had dulled my judgment.

Going to the police didn't cross my mind until the next day when Three Piece called me repeatedly. I ignored his calls and couldn't understand why he would try to contact me. I was at work and unable to concentrate because I felt the trauma of the previous night all over again.

But he continued to try to reach me. When I did finally take his call, I managed to seethe through my clinched teeth "What - do - you - want?! Why are you calling me?! I can't believe you have the nerve to call me after what you did!" It was almost a whisper, but I managed to convey my total disgust, anger, and feelings of betrayal. I didn't want to cause a scene at work.

He began to apologize and say he was sorry. He didn't mean anything bad towards me. He wasn't trying to hurt me. "Baby, you are fine, and I just wanted you. Didn't you want me too?" Truth is, physically, he was exactly the kind of man I wanted. That's where my desire for him ended. The thought of a big, strong man is appealing. Strong in body with his strength centered in God; a strong gentleness. But there seemed to be no gentle man in him. I only saw him as a savage willing to devour me without my consent. His assessment of me could not have been more incorrect.

What I wanted was a man so passionate about God and the order of what God intended for us that he would recognize that same passion for God in me. Eventually we would walk as one. We'd experience the passion God intended for couples to have. Sounds lofty but it was and remains what I desire. That type of passion doesn't happen on date number two with one party screaming, "No! Don't."

As shocking as the attack was, it didn't dawn on me that I should involve the police in the matter. Many years later when I recounted this event to a loved one, they asked what happened to Three Piece and how could I move on after being traumatized? When I talked to him the day after the assault, I never wanted to talk or think of him again. To that sentiment, I ended the call with this promise, "If you ever, ever try to contact me again, EVER, I will get the police involved! Lose my number and forget you met me!!!"

The reality of the situation was that I also blamed myself. I had chosen to ignore the rules of common sense and was repaid with an assault. I knew ultimately that he was at fault, but I felt and believed I had contributed. The shame of that realization kept me silent for years. I had already beat myself up about my situational stupidity. I couldn't imagine revealing my missteps to the authorities and also facing their rebuke. The stigma attached to "victim" just wasn't me. I didn't and still don't identify as a victim. Attacks like mine go unreported more often than anyone can estimate. Unfortunately, I know from experience.

~ ~ ~

A year or so later, I dusted myself off and proceeded with caution. Resuming the search with my little voice and common sense in tow, I gingerly re-entered the pool. I got back on the horse. I could stay frozen in the trauma of that horrible night or move past it. I chose to move forward.

The newly evolved Lyn would do things right. Following the safety rules I had put in place was a crucial part of trying again. The smarter version of myself reviewed my potential applicants through a different lens. I got a little better at reading between the lines and understanding what wasn't on the page.

Taking Applications

Patriotic Paul

Taking Applications

Marching Forward
Patriotic Paul

I had a few dates prior to meeting Patriotic Paul; however, I had been going through the motions with timidity. I had decided to get back to the search but understandably was a little reserved and not my true fun-loving self. I refused to be stuck in fear. I needed to adopt a better outlook and declared, "If I'm gonna do this, I'm gonna do this and have a good time!" I'd be bold and step outside of my box... safely... and have fun.

Patriotic Paul would be one of the rewards of dusting myself off. We had several conversations over the dating app and decided to take our conversations to the personal email level. Prior to that, I had learned that he was a believer, loved dogs, and was prior military. I had recently taken a position supporting the military and felt we'd have that "God, Country, Service" vibe built in. It also didn't hurt my head that he was tall, dark, and handsome to boot or so his profile said.

Confirmation that we'd hit it off came when I saw his email address: marrynomore@whatever. We spoke the same language in this area. Although I was searching again, I still had reservations. The pain of a failed marriage and the incident with Three Piece had long-lasting affects. I didn't trust my ability to choose a life partner yet. I had convinced myself that I didn't want to get married just yet. Patriotic Paul was advertising through his email address that he didn't want to get married. Okay, good. I just wanted a friend that could turn into something more… eventually. We could talk without the stress of thinking about long-term commitments. We could get to know each other and have fun. I wouldn't have to worry about making the mistake of marrying the wrong guy again. He was safe.

When Patriotic Paul asked for our first outing to be the zoo, I swallowed my personal opinion about the zoo and cheerfully accepted the invitation. Although I'd been to the zoo many times, it was not my favorite place to be. Enduring the smells were not my idea of a fun time. Growing up, I had been exposed to the weekly animal kingdom programs giving me an appreciation for animals of all kinds. I made sure my sons were also exposed, especially since my older son was a die-hard animal lover. I had taken them to the Wild Animal Park in San Diego as well as the Los Angeles Zoo. Paul's love and enthusiasm for animals caused me to suppress my dislike for the zoo.

My step outside of my box attitude paid off. We had a great time walking around the zoo and getting to know each other. I found out he especially loved bears and wanted one, a real one, not a teddy bear. He literally joked with me about making friends with the bear in front of us. The bears were in one of those natural habitat environments, which made me fear

Paul would actually try to climb into the area as he threatened.

After the zoo, we caught a bite to eat at a nearby restaurant. Conversation with him was easy. Hmm, I thought. This is good. We must have talked for a couple of hours. Feeling a little guilty for taking up our waitress's table for so long, we moved the conversation to the parking lot. We continued talking for a couple more hours and decided we should go out again. I was on cloud nine. We had so much in common and really seemed to be having reciprocal feelings for each other.

~ ~ ~

He would tease me mercilessly about my pancake eating rituals.

~ ~ ~

Paul showed me he had a crazy sense of humor and would say whatever came to his mind without filter. It was the same quality I had been repeatedly chided for exhibiting when I was a child. It was refreshing to be able to freely express myself without fear of judgment. He would often crack up laughing at something I probably shouldn't have said. I would innocently exclaim, "What?! What did I say?!" In turn, I thought he might have a screw or two loose based upon some of his antics.

He would tease me mercilessly about my pancake eating rituals. On our first visit to IHOP, we were enjoying our conversation and waiting for our orders to be delivered to the table. We talked and laughed about this and that until the order came. I looked down at my plate and tried to hide my disappointment at the sight of my pancakes. I silently tried to spread my cold butter before cutting them into perfect little squares. Paul noticed my change in demeanor and asked, "What's wrong?" "Nothing," I whispered. "No, really, what's wrong?" I stuttered a bit and said, "My pancakes have a hole in them." He interrupted, "What? Your pancakes have a hole?" "Yes, and I can't spread my butter. It's tearing my pancakes." He then began to mock me in the voice of a very proper elderly British lady, "Her pancakes have a hole and she can't spread her butter. Please pass the Grey Poupon, Miss." He had me laughing so hard and realizing how silly I was being over my pancakes. Occasionally, Paul would whip out that phrase to lighten the mood when I'd start stressing over something small or insignificant. He'd also order my butter on the side for my pancakes (smile). Humor and laughter were big in our relationship.

Several dates in, Paul decided to take it to the next level and introduced me to his babies. He had three and they were the loves of his life. His babies were his dogs: Kleo, Goldie, and Paz; two Rottweilers and a Chocolate Labrador. As I entered his place, I was met by one of the biggest Rottweilers I'd ever seen. Thankfully, Paz was in an enclosure that I wasn't sure would hold him should he decide he didn't like me. I would find out later that Paz had no idea that he was a giant dog and could just push or jump over the enclosure and be free. Although he looked like a beast, Paz was a teddy bear of a dog and well trained by Paul who also added certified dog trainer to his list of talents.

Kleo, the other Rottweiler, took one look at me and immediately marked the moment with a growl of mistrust. I could have sworn she gave me the side eye. Paul assured me that she was just a little territorial when it came to anyone showing him attention. "Ah, she's in charge of the house?" I surmised. "Very much so," he told me. When I hugged Paul, she would go off the rails barking. However, Goldie, the Labrador, wanted to make friends right away. As soon as Kleo gave her the go-ahead, Goldie came over to buddy up to me. She was the sweetest, friendliest dog. To Paul's wonder, his babies would embrace his new friend. After a while, even Kleo came around and would initiate getting some affection from me.

After introducing me to his dogs, he excused himself and said, "I'll be right back. I want to show you something." Through our getting to know each other, I learned he had served our country for nearly twenty years and had completed two tours of duty in the Middle East. He was a Veteran and had decided to introduce me to his other babies, his firearms. We had talked about them on the phone, but I hadn't expected to see them. He came back in the room and proudly displayed them on the table. Patriotic Paul was military through and through. I was full of questions. He patiently explained what each one was and the safety measures that must always be observed. Although my brother and brother-in-law were both retired police officers, I had very little hands-on exposure with guns.

My apprehension gave way to respect and understanding as Paul began to break down the weapon and recite what he would explain is the gun (rifleman) creed (in part):

"This is my gun. There are many like it, but this one is mine. My gun is my best friend. It is my life. I must master it as I must master my life. Without me, my gun

is useless. Without my gun, I am useless. I must fire my gun true. I must shoot straighter than my enemy who is trying to kill me. My gun is human, even as I, because it is my life. Thus, I will learn it as a brother.

I will learn its weaknesses, its strength, its parts, its accessories, its sights and its barrel. I will keep my gun clean and ready, even as I am clean and ready. We will become part of each other. Before God, I swear this creed. My gun and I are the defenders of my country. We are the masters of our enemy. We are the saviors of my life. So be it, until victory is America's and there is no enemy, but peace!"

He had gone into "the zone" while reciting the creed. It was quite impressive and a very clear exercise in the dedication Paul embodied and exhibited in his service to our country. It was clear to me that he was opening up and exposing himself to me. Getting to see his serious, military, and macho side was endearing. I could relate to his dedication and commitment. It was another set of characteristics we shared. My own work with the military was a very cherished period of my life. I continue to have a very strong connection and love for my military family.

I was having fun with this man. Paul had me thinking about love again. By this time, Three Piece and a Face Rag was a distant memory. I marched forward with a new cadence to my life. Paul and I continued to get to know each other. We spent more and more time living in each other's worlds until they began to mesh into a comfortable "our world" rhythm.

Taking Applications

He accompanied me to work-related events and impressed me with his interactions with my peers and more so with the commanding officers I supported. This total man's man exhibited intelligence and class without missing a beat. He was gallant without effort. It was so appealing to me. I was completely smitten.

Paul fit right in with my family too. Of course, he was teased mercilessly about being the third Paul. He'd just quip something back like, "It took her three tries to get it right," or "She saved the best for last."

I can't recall when the transition in my brain and heart happened. I was falling in love with this man. That was not supposed to happen I told myself. Paul seemed to be feeling the same thing, but I wasn't sure. The more time I spent with him, the more time I wanted to spend with him. My heart was humming and on the verge of singing. We were very supportive of each other's feelings, desires, dreams, and everyday lives. Our communication was pretty good. The strangest thing in our relationship was the absence of major conflicts. In hindsight, painting Paul as perfect is not my intention, nevertheless, he was a definite keeper in my mind.

I wanted him fully. When I met Paul, he told me that he didn't want to get married. I felt the same way until I realized I was in love with him. My feelings had changed. By this time, he had already confessed he loved me too. I, however, wanted more; needed more. I flipped the script; I wanted to settle down and get married. We were more than a year in at this point. Why stay single when love strikes again? There seemed to be zero reasons why we wouldn't take the next step.

This became my contention with him. He wanted things to remain the same. "No need to mess up a good thing. Let's just keep things as they are," he'd say. So, we'd keep things as they were and continued to enjoy our relationship. He was preoccupied with making millions and caring for his fur babies. Marrying me was not even on his vision board. Instead there was a picture of Beyoncé and him in another photo next to her with his arm extended like it was actually around her. There were houses, cars, and other luxury items; but, not one picture of me. When I pointed it out, he just replied, "You know how I feel about you. You're my girl." And I'd say, "Then why is Beyoncé up there and not me?" He'd have no answer.

Every few months or so, I'd get frustrated at keeping things the same and would approach the subject with Paul. He would not budge on this point. He failed to see that I was looking for validation of his love. I didn't want to be the eternal girlfriend. I longed to hear the ultimate words of validation: "I love you. Will you spend the rest of your life with me? Marry me, Babe!" It was not to be.

To complicate how I felt deep in my heart, there was always some woman flirting with him and he seemed to thrive off of the attention. He did not put up clear boundaries. We knew what we had was good but sometimes other women didn't respect that since he didn't put up a big fat stop sign. I sometimes doubted myself and wondered if maybe he just didn't want to marry me specifically and I was just a placeholder until he found his Beyoncé.

I had changed and wanted more. He didn't agree. It seemed the more I expressed I wanted more, the more he dug into his status quo position. His first marriage had been a nightmare and his parent's example of marriage had convinced him that he should never put himself in that position again. Meanwhile, I was the hope-filled romantic that wanted to grow old together hand in hand. We'd conquer the world together. And... we did for a while.

"What are you doing, Miss?" I'd reply, "Oh nothing, just looking for the "S" on your chest."

Although Paul had retired from the military, he continued to be the hero to so many people in his everyday life, sometimes to the point of forgetting about the quiet folks not in need of an immediate rescue or attention. I often teased him and would feign an inspection of sorts by looking under his shirt. He would say, "What are you doing, Miss?" I'd reply, "Oh nothing, just looking for the "S" on your chest." My Clark Kent retired Navy man was just a phone call away for those needing this or that. Every now and then I'd accompany him on one of his missions. I considered myself his Lois Lane. Sometimes being Lois could get a little dangerous (if only in my mind).

I recall a particularly memorable dinner Paul invited me to attend with him. He had been working diligently to get his real estate and investing ventures off the ground. Part of the networking circles he traveled in would get together with potential investors to casually introduce them to real estate investing through a game called Cash Flow 101. The game is very similar to Monopoly but with more realistic applications of real estate strategies. Paul had been invited to dinner and to introduce the game to some friends and he invited me to tag along.

Prior to the dinner, I wondered to myself if the host knew he was bringing me along because I suspected one of the women attending had a crush on Paul. When I asked him had he told her friend that I was coming, he assured me that the woman, Brianna, only had business interest in him and wouldn't care if I attended. But my intuition was telling me a completely different story. She seemed a little overzealous when it came to anything Paul was doing.

We arrived at the host's apartment at the appointed time. My suspicions were immediately confirmed. As Paul introduced me to the host, Mary, and her friend, Brianna, I could feel the tension right away. Brianna's look of disappointment was so obvious. The two women had been preparing dinner and were trying to put the finishing touches on the meal. Brianna was so upset at Paul's surprise guest that she left the room almost immediately. Mary pulled Paul into another room to confront him about me. She told him Brianna thought that she and Paul were dating and why did he bring me? Furthermore, she wanted to know, "Why does Brianna think you are dating her? Have you been leading her on? What's going on?"

Paul was stunned. He explained to Mary that he thought Brianna wanted to know about real estate. "All of our interactions have been about business. She's been asking me about the Cash Flow game and has been asking me to show her properties. That's all I've done. I don't know why she would even think that." I had tried to warn him that her interest in real estate had been a cover to get close to him, but he thought I was being overly sensitive or jealous. I'm fairly laid back when it comes to these things. I figured he'd see it in due time.

A big clue to her tactics was on one occasion when they viewed some property. After which, she urgently needed to use the bathroom and asked if they could stop by his place since they were in his neighborhood. They did stop (which he told me about later) and she tried to stay and hang out. According to him, he cut that short and informed her he had another appointment. I would later tell him that he missed a perfect opportunity to tell her about us. He didn't think that would be a good business decision.

Meanwhile, everyone left me in the room alone while they dealt with the surprise drama. I was left standing in the small kitchen/dining/living area to figure out what to do. I could hear Paul and Mary talking quietly. When Mary and Paul returned, Mary offered me something to drink. She said dinner was almost ready and the other couple had called to say they would be there soon. Quietly, I asked Paul what was going on. "Brianna's in the bathroom crying and Mary wanted to know the 411. I'll explain later," he whispered. It was a very small apartment. Having a detailed conversation was not really a good option.

A few minutes later, Brianna returned to help Mary finish the meal preparations. It was obvious she had been crying. I felt for her but was insistent on making sure she had no doubt that I was his woman. Just an aside: I generally feel like it's the man's job to put clear boundaries up when doing business with women. In this instance, I was fully engaged in marking my territory in the nicest of ways. I could already see that she was crushed. There was no need to rub it in. Brianna, however, hadn't fully given up.

The other couple arrived and introductions were made all around. A few telling looks were exchanged but I acted as though everything was normal. It was one of those "if looks could kill" moments. When Mary and Brianna set the table, there wasn't room for six at the table. Brianna decided to set a place for me in the living room area... alone. She had conveniently seated Paul next to her at the table. We prayed over the meal and dinner began. I had to silently laugh when Paul politely picked up his place setting, came to the couch where I was seated, and sat down to eat. I thought Brianna was going to start crying again but she held it together. Even though Paul sat next to me, I was still a little miffed with him for causing the uncomfortable scene. I was afraid to eat my food for fear that she may have given me a little something extra. But we got through the meal unscathed, cleared the dishes, and set up for the Cash Flow game. Since Paul is such a likable person and full of jokes, the tension in the room eased somewhat once we set up the game and played a while. Even Brianna seemed to lighten up a little. She didn't stop staring me down but managed to keep it to a minimum or maybe I stopped noticing.

I was so glad when that evening was over and we got out

of there. Paul and I had some serious discussions on the forensics of how that evening's events came to be. It was a night mixed with so much drama, sadness, misunderstanding, comedy, and major lessons learned. Not surprisingly, Brianna lost interest in real estate and never did invest when it became clear that what she really wanted to invest in was not available to her. Besides, she wasn't his Beyoncé. Paul really needed to remove the "S" from his chest.

I included that story because it was one illustration of his failure to set boundaries. Time would pass and it would repeat with some other woman. Paul's no boundaries issue, my desire to take our relationship to the next level, and his insistence that nothing change would eventually cause me to walk away. I knew who and what I wanted but he didn't want the same thing. He didn't want me forever. I felt rejected. Giving up on such a promising man who had grabbed my heart was nearly impossible. Paul and I shared so many major goals and beliefs. In addition to the big things, we had many of the elements that make a relationship truly special. We had chemistry, passion, laughter, conversation, friendship, and we just enjoyed being with each other.

But I would make a life-altering decision for our relationship. We went to dinner at one of my favorite restaurants, The Cheesecake Factory, in Sherman Oaks. All throughout dinner, I contemplated what I was about to do. As usual, we were having a good time together. I didn't think I was going to be able to go through with what I thought I needed to say. I asked myself, Why are you gonna rock this boat? Why can't you just be satisfied with just this? I vacillated back and forth in my head but felt I had no other option.

After dinner, we walked hand in hand through the plaza talking. I suppressed my immense emotions and fought back the tears of my broken heart. Before I'd even spoken a word, I was mourning the loss. After almost four years, I took a deep breath and I began to explain that I really wanted more of us on a permanent basis. I expressed my understanding that he did not echo my sentiments and had no plans to change his position. I told him that we should just break-up and call it quits. Paul was quiet. He seemed surprised and subdued but didn't stop me nor try to persuade me against a break-up. I was very distraught and couldn't read his take on my announcement. I can't recall his exact words; it was all a blur after I said we should break up. Paul didn't fight for me. He had taken the "S" off of his chest and didn't try to rescue me. He had no clue that I had been drowning and needed his rescue more than anyone he'd ever saved.

Secretly I had hoped walking away would spur him into action to ask me to be his wife. It did spur him into action, but it wasn't the action I expected. He would start a relationship with someone else right away. The fact that he chose a woman who had been aggressively flirting with him (not Brianna) for more than a year unchecked was excruciating. Here I was in hurt city again. What had I done? I shouldn't have ended our relationship. It was not a game. Playing games was not in my wheelhouse. I was always a what you see is what you get kind of person and generally wore my heart on my sleeve. I just felt I had to do something. I didn't want to be the eternal girlfriend. I wanted to be his wife and conquer the world together.

I had opened myself up to Paul. I was completely vulnerable. But I had given up and walked away. Where was my romance novel happy ending? It wasn't to be. I thought he'd come around to my way of thinking if I loved him hard enough. I've often felt that my feelings for him were much stronger than his feelings for me. The reality was that the unequal emotions between us was not healthy for me. It was confusing. I continued to fall into his patterns of attraction and then his pulling away when feelings were too intense for him. The singer Bonnie Raitt had it right when she sang, "I can't make you love me if you don't." My optimistic nature had blinded me to the truth that he did not love me. He had strong feelings perhaps, but it was not love. True acceptance of that fact was elusive.

Oddly, we salvaged a friendship. I'm not sure exactly how this came to be, but it was a pattern I had repeated with my significant ex's. My relationships always ended on friendly terms, sometimes too friendly. It hurt not to be with Paul but at least I could still hear his laugh from time to time and just talk. And talk we did. He'd share about the woes of his new relationship and I'd think to myself, You're a glutton for punishment. Why are you letting him vent to you about her? Is this really a friendship or am I secretly thinking we'll get back together? Is it really worth it remaining this close to him? It was time to move forward and get over him… for real. I needed to cut ties. In spite of my still attached heart, that's what I set out to do.

Life moves on. Time passes.

Taking Applications

Man Down... But Not Out

After the break-up, I slipped into my old childhood feelings of not measuring up no matter how hard I tried. My perfectionist father's insistence that I be perfect haunted me. I flashed back to my teen years and showing him my report card. I'd rush to deliver my grades. I was proud of my four A's and two B's, but his response was, "Why didn't you get all A's?" Or the times I would bring home medals earned in city and state competitions for flute performances. He'd have very little response and would barely acknowledge my accomplishments. I could never impress him. If I did impress him, he never gave me a clue he was pleased with me. His critical voice would replay in my head for the rest of my life. I tore myself apart dissecting every flaw in my personality and physical appearance.

My strength would come when I'd refocus my attention on the reality of who I really was. Through all of my years of studying the Bible, I had learned that God had created, loved, and accepted me just as I am. I had to stop listening to the negative repeating tape of my earthly father and embrace the reality of God the Father's love. I am enough! I am loved!

Lyn Noble

Taking Applications

Give Up? Not Me

It wasn't overnight that I wanted to try again. But, eventually, I did want to try. As a hope-filled optimist, I wanted to walk in and say, "Lucy, I'm home." Well, not Lucy, but you get my meaning. I still had the desire to be someone's special someone. It was time for action. Nothing ventured, nothing gained.

The ordinary channels of meeting men didn't seem to be working for me. I was always meeting people but not in the right situations. It was mostly through church or work that I'd meet new men. Most of the men in church my age were married or not good candidates for me. The men at work were completely off-limits.

Alas, I was back to taking applications. At first, I didn't really have my heart in the renewed search. But going out with other people helped to get my mind off of Patriotic Paul. For several years after him, I would browse profiles and compare the potential dates to Paul number two and three. Both of them were outstanding men with great characteristics, not perfect, but really good men. I missed them both. I didn't realize I had made them the measuring standard for men I'd meet, but I had. I have often joked that I'd have my perfect match if I Frankenstein'd my ex's together.

I had a few unremarkable dates where nothing went terribly wrong nor anything particularly noteworthy happened. There were a few more along the way who would be around long enough to earn nicknames like Dan the Man Without a Plan and Big G. And of course, there was another Paul that I had the hugest crush on (What?! It's a popular name).

The physical attraction with this Paul was extremely strong on both sides but he didn't share my faith. He was tall (6'4"), dark mocha, and very handsome. We went out on a few dates where it was obvious that there was no shortage of physical chemistry. I didn't trust myself alone with him because of this. After all, I was practicing celibacy and we all know what happens when you're practicing something. You make mistakes. My nagging lusty thoughts and physical attraction to him consciously made me be cautious and guarded. The relationship just never seemed to gain enough momentum to be long lasting. In the end, I might have been a little too conservative and square for him since I never gave him a clue to my internal dialog.

~ ~ ~
My organized mind couldn't seem to understand his "wing it at all times, let's just see what happens" strategy in life.
~ ~ ~

Dan the Man was not a right fit from the beginning; however, he seemed to think I would be a perfect mate for him. He'd try to convince me by saying, "I'm looking for a Christian woman. You're a Christian, check. You're into music, check.

Combine the two, you're in music ministry, check. You're cute, check. So go out with me. Let me take you out to dinner. Come on, you gotta eat." He had good reasoning. Although I wasn't attracted to him in any way, on paper, he was right; it seemed like a good match. Dan's persistence won out and he talked me into going out with him. I said to myself, It won't hurt to go out with him once. Don't be so quick to reject his interest.

Instead of a one time date, I actually ended up spending a considerable amount of time with him over the next few months. I'd tell myself I didn't want to spend any more time with him but would do it anyway. Why did I do that? I'd ask myself. Maybe I was in a low self-esteem period or something. In spite of my non-feelings for him, I'd find myself hanging out with him again. I had firmly put him in the friend zone. I don't think that was fair to him but it's what I did.

My organized mind couldn't seem to understand his "wing it at all times, let's just see what happens" strategy in life. It was especially discouraging when we were involved in a big project that required the logistics to be on point. Watching unnecessary chaos due to poor planning or no planning at all was like dragging fingernails on a chalkboard. Surprisingly, I love to plan things; like everything. However, having your guy plan out special times is really cool. I had been spoiled by Music Paul and his ability to make moments happen. Dan's annoying trait coupled with the no attraction thing helped designate him into the friend only zone. Dan persistently tried to move into my heart zone… unsuccessfully.

In hindsight, I took the responsibility for this relationship not working out. I could tell by our initial phone calls that there was no chemistry on my end. I should have just said no thank you during what I've deemed my loneliness period. Lesson learned: Stick to your guns... listen to your inner voice.

~ ~ ~

Big G would also be someone I'd spend too much time with knowing that he was not the one for me. He sounded so much like my Caribbean ex-husband and his real name was too similar to one of my brother's names. It just felt weird to call my brother's name to someone who was trying to be a love interest. The whole cool accent and laid-back attitude felt like a déjà vu of my ex-husband. I had been a sucker for an accent.

Nevertheless, we would go out occasionally as just friends; I was very clear on that point. He would still flirt like crazy and ask me to be his wife... every time. It was cute; but he was not a keeper. At times I would play with the idea of making him more than a friend, but he would earn a couple of bad strikes against him early on that would shatter that vapor of a thought and any other ideas of hanging out with him at all.

The first time we went to dinner we had a nice time. It was at a little diner. The food was decent and the service good. We had pleasant conversation and laughed a lot. I thought the date had gone well although I was weirded out by the aforementioned accent and my brother's name thing. When it came time to pay the bill, Big G did not leave the waitress a tip. I tried to let him be him, I just couldn't though. The waitress had done a good job and deserved a good tip. When I have it to give, I am a habitual over tipper. Naturally, it would bother me to see him stiff this hard-working woman. When I asked him why he didn't leave her a tip, he replied that it was because of her race. I was livid. I immediately returned to the restaurant, found the waitress, and personally handed her a tip. Then, I addressed the ugliness with my new "friend." After talking with him at length about his reasoning of that nonsense, he apologized and said he was wrong. I was not totally convinced that his apology was sincere. It felt more like he told me what he thought I wanted to hear. He had shown me his true colors. It was a turn off and I didn't want to pursue any type of romantic relationship.

He continued to call me. After numerous apologies, as usual, I softened, forgave his bad behavior, and went out with him as a friend only. He told me he was gonna change my mind on that. The second deadly strike, however, totally killed that deal too. Nobody's perfect, especially not me. However, there are a few things that no one should allow in a relationship: violence, habitual lying, cheating, and other common-sense no-nos. Then there are other lessor offenses like standing your date up and completely ghosting without a trace.

After our initial date, I had moved on to date others (without much success) but he continued to call. When I decided to let it progress past his relentless flirting and try actually dating him seriously the incident happened. We had a bona fide date planned. Due to my schedule, we were going to meet at the location. At the appointed time I was there waiting, waiting, and more waiting. I checked the time. After about 20 minutes I called him; no answer. I waited another 15 to 20 minutes; still no show. Then I began to worry. He wasn't one to be late. He never stood me up before. In fact, I had never been stood up at all; it was uncharted territory. Perhaps he had been caught up in traffic and his cell phone died. After an hour of waiting and calling, I left and went home. I continued to call him that evening thinking something had happened to him. It didn't dawn on me that he had just stood me up. It had taken me almost two years to let him in and then he just stood me up, just like that.

A few days later, he called as if nothing had happened. When I asked where he had been and why didn't he show up, his response was that he was going through something and that he was sorry. With unmasked anger, I said, "And you didn't have the decency to call to let me know you couldn't make it?" He repeated his apology that he was really going through something tough and didn't want to burden me with it. I countered back that I thought something tragic had happened to him since I had received zero responses to messages I had left him. To this day, I think he had someone else or went "on vacation" or something. Nevertheless, he stood me up. Dating him after that became a non-issue.

… Movies and a lot of flirting; that was it.

Taking Applications

SC with the Immaculately Conceived Son

I never gave up on the Christian sites. This time I chose and met up with my faith-filled date at the local Guitar Center. Let's call him SC, short for Super Christian. The music store was his Friday night hang-out spot. He played keys (mostly jazz) and was in the market for a new keyboard. He asked if I would help him choose one? "Sure, music geeks unite." I was off to the store in my jeans and positive, bubbly attitude. This was definitely an unusual first date, but I always enjoyed hanging out in the keyboard room playing the electric pianos and keyboards for hours. If we didn't like each other, it would just be about the music.

Why does the Christian musician get a mention in the book? I'm glad you asked. My perceptions of what I expected people to be was based on what they said or tried to project. It was sometimes skewed by my own life experiences. I will generally give people the benefit of the doubt until they prove otherwise. Until then, there is a lot of grace happening. Just like I've been shown grace by God, I figured that I should do the same. SC would be over the top and would require extra grace.

Let me explain... no, let me summarize. It's appropriate to say up front that this man really pursued me. He was the ultimate gentlemen and generally fun to hang out with. We would spend a lot of time getting to know one another usually over a really good meal. SC was a bit of a foodie. He knew all of the great casual food spots around the greater L.A. area. Actually, he was knowledgeable about many subjects. I liked that about him.

He liked to talk; we had that in common. He could be a good listener at times. Having someone to discuss faith and the concerns of day-to-day life from that perspective was a plus. Our discussions on the Bible were extensive. He had studied and had in-depth knowledge. I had also taken my fair share of advanced classes and study groups over the years. To say that the discussions could be exhaustive would be putting it lightly. I rather enjoy studying and discussions on the topic, however, too many times a simple question or statement turned into a one-sided 20-minute lecture from him. It wasn't an exchange of ideas, more like a mini sermon. It was annoying. I longed for open dialog about God and faith, not to be talked at on and on.

After months of getting to know SC, he revealed that although he was really into me, we should probably stop seeing each other. He explained that it was wrong to be dating me because I had been previously married thus it would be adulterous. "What?!" I said, not understanding what he could possibly be trying to say. On my profile, my status was clearly stated along with the fact that I had children (grown by that time). My marital status was not new information that had just come to light.

I was puzzled and waited for him to explain which of course he did. He took me to a passage in the Bible. The only problem was when I reminded him that although he had never been married, he also had a son the same age as my younger son. "How does that work exactly? You have a son out of wedlock which would also be considered adultery by your own explanation of the passage? That would mean you could never be married? Unless, your son was conceived immaculately," I sarcastically concluded. In my opinion, it was a gross misinterpretation of the Word, but I agreed to disagree with him on the point. SC was the one who had expressed interest in me with full knowledge of who I was. It was strange to hear his fervent explanations. I wasn't crushed by his revelation. His super-duper over the top pseudo-Christian philosophy had already been rubbing me the wrong way.

However, he had thrown me a curve ball. Just a few weeks before this conversation, SC had taken me on a mystery date. He had planned the day out but hadn't given me details. "Wear something comfortable. We're going for a drive. I want to show you something special," he said. We drove up to a park on the shores of the Palos Verdes area which has absolutely beautiful vista views. We stood at the bluff and took it all in. He held my hand and we talked about how God had created such beauty. We were awestruck. It was remarkably picturesque and romantic.

He then drove us to Wayfarers Chapel, the little glass chapel, also in Palos Verdes. The chapel is breathtakingly beautiful and charming. The building is predominately constructed of glass and is surrounded by lush gardens and tall trees. SC explained that it was designed by the famous architect Lloyd Wright. He went on to tell me people came from all over the world to get married there. The grounds-keeper had been cleaning up from an event (a wedding) and allowed us into the chapel. SC talked about how he could serenade me on keys and how beautiful the acoustics were. Although our relationship had not advanced to the level of thinking of marriage, he surely had taken me on what seemed like a romantic, let's get more serious date. I even wondered whether he was planning to propose. By the way, I did not want him to.

But back to the breakup, if we want to completely call it that. Because interestingly enough, much like other ex-boyfriends, we stayed in touch. He would occasionally call and invite me to join him for dinner because he was going to be in the area. Sometimes, I'd accept and we would have a good time. That is until he would ask my advice on things happening in his life regarding the woman he was dating. The new girlfriend happened to be about twenty years his junior. Perhaps he had just decided to trade me in for a younger model but missed having adult conversation.

Okay, that was a little mean but probably true (rolling my eyes).

Taking Applications

A Different Adventure

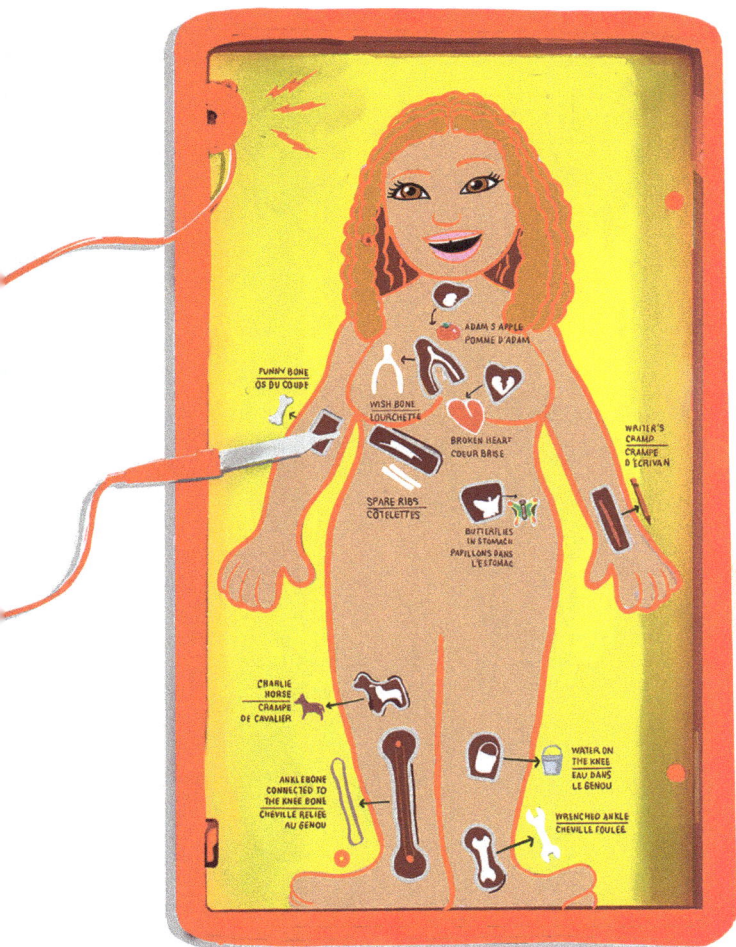

Taking Applications

A Different Adventure

Subsequently, I'd be very distracted by my own new drama. Thoughts of dating had to be put on the back burner. I had been working long hours at L.A. Air Force Base and was days away from semester finals in a Pace program at Pierce College. I was determined to finish the semester with continued Dean's List status without missing a beat at work. I was exhausted and had come down with what I thought was a cold. It was clearly not a cold since I passed out on my way back to my desk at work. When I came to a few seconds later, there was a flurry of activity around me. I could hear talking about 911, the hospital and blah, blah, blah… As I gathered my bearings, I got to my feet and sat in my chair. I told them I was okay and didn't need to go to the hospital; I was just tired and had a bad cold.

By this time, my team lead had arrived and insisted, along with everyone else, that I go to the hospital. Off to the hospital I was taken. The doctors would determine I had a serious staph infection along with alarmingly elevated glucose levels which required immediate treatment . They stabilized me, doped me up, and eventually sent me home later that evening. In addition to the diagnosed staph infection, I had also been suffering with major back pain that radiated down the length of my leg and affected my ability to stand, sit, or walk without cringing in pain. I figured I had just been pushing myself too hard; burning the candle at both ends and maybe the middle too.

~ ~ ~

It was an extraordinarily stressful time...

~ ~ ~

While testing for the origin of the back/leg pain issues, my primary doctor decided I should also have some other medical tests conducted. Being a diabetic meant I should have regular checkups on my eyes and feet. He threw in a mammogram for good measure. I obediently complied with all of his testing requests. All three tests would require additional attention; the most pressing being the mammogram results. The resulting cancer diagnosis took priority over everything else. My regular hectic life came to an abrupt halt and a new journey began. A whirlwind of medical testing, explanations, options on possible procedures, and decisions ensued. I would spend the next year and a half dealing with just the cancer.

It was an extraordinarily stressful and trying time. I had lost my mom a couple of years earlier, and two other siblings had passed from cancer. Cancer had hit my family hard. I was commuting from the valley to the South Bay area, over an hour each way, for my own treatment. I felt isolated and alone. Although I talked on the phone to them, most of my family and friends lived far away. I felt extremely vulnerable and if I'm completely candid, I was lonely. My faith was my strength and how I kept a positive attitude. I recall a time after the second breast cancer surgery when I wanted a break from the constant strain of dealing with the medical stuff. I decided to escape to the movies for a couple of hours. I have a quirky habit of not wanting to see movie trailers before seeing the movie. I want the story to unfold without the prompts commercials and trailers reveal. I don't want to know the story details. This practice usually works out well for me; not so much this time. A matinée was showing at Sherman Oaks Galleria of the movie 50/50 starring Joseph Gordon-Levitt. I bought a small popcorn (I was being good) and took my seat. The theatre was empty. I would later be happy about that. As the movie develops, it turns out the main character played by Gordon-Levitt has cancer and is dealing with treatment mostly alone despite his request for his girlfriend's support. What are the odds of going to see a movie to escape thinking about cancer and then facing a cancer themed movie? I boo-hoo cried like a little baby. I did not have enough tissues and napkins to handle the flood of tears. It was an ugly cry session that resulted in a red nose and very puffy eyes. It wasn't quite the escape I was going for, but it was definitely cathartic.

Every now and then during my recovery, I'd get bored, look at the dating sites, and think about the day I'd be well again. It was nothing but a fantasy and distraction at that point since the only dates I could have were with a bevy of doctors and my nurse who came to re-dress my surgical wounds daily. It was a chapter in my life that was more like a novel. I don't really dwell on it. That's a different story for another time.

Let's move on because the journey continued.

Taking Applications

Back to Will

Taking Applications

Back to Will

"Hi, I just heard your voice mail messages. You sounded so worried. I thought I should let you know that I'm in the hospital." I hadn't told him I had been dealing with anything other than the cancer which was in check. Will had lost his wife to cancer. "They're running some tests," I continued. "Oh wow! Are you okay?" he asked, "What hospital?" Next thing I knew, Will appeared in my hospital room with a box of candy and a card. He didn't know candy was on my no-no list. This was the first time he had laid eyes on me in person; in the hospital, in a hospital gown. What had I been thinking to tell him that I was in the hospital? I was dealing with another medical scare and had been in the hospital for a couple of days. Who knew that Will would drop everything and come see about me? Ignoring my protest of him coming to the hospital, he had said, "I was so worried about you! I've been leaving you messages. I had to come see about my baby!"

Prior to this, we had been corresponding via the site, email, phone, and text. We had not met in person. I was still dealing with some lingering medical issues and didn't really want to take it to that level yet. Most of my focus was on getting completely well. Will had been sending me inspirational messages and posting songs on my page for months. Admittedly, I ignored them at first because I thought he was a big flirt. I could see the other traffic on his profile page. He had many women leaving him messages and flirts. I was only window shopping and also didn't want to be a part of his Internet harem.

I have jokingly blamed Judge Milian for my meeting Will. I was watching People's Court and trying to stay still while the nurse who came in daily to change my surgical dressing did her thing. There was a woman suing a man over a loan she had extended him. Judge Milian picked up on a vibe between the plaintiff and defendant and asked them, "Are you two dating?" They confirmed that they had dated. The judge went on to ask how long and were they still together? She wanted to know how they had met. One of them said they met on Tagged. Judge Milian asked, "What is Tagged?" The woman explained it's a social media site. "Well actually it's a dating site," she confessed. I had never heard of Tagged, was curious, and checked it out and encountered Will. There you have it. It's all Judge Milian's fault (big smile).

~ ~ ~
I gave up some of the control over my life and accepted him into my heart.
~ ~ ~

That first gentlemanly gesture/hospital visit endeared Will to me. It was such a sweet move. He had been sending me daily inspirational messages for several months like clockwork. At a time when things had been extremely stressful, it meant a lot to me that he dropped what he was doing and was there by my side. My little birdie voice that had been telling me Will was a player and a bad boy had been silenced by his outpouring of compassion. It was a strange way to start out, but aren't the strangest situations sometimes the sweetest? It was an emotionally vulnerable time for me and I let my guard down. All the pieces were in place for me to make decisions I never would have previously made. I gave up some of the control over my life and accepted him into my heart. My heart wasn't singing but that didn't matter. I had someone who cared about me and what I was going through. He wasn't scared away by the cancer that was in remission, nor any of the other issues I faced. That hospital stay was short and I was cleared to go home.

Will and I started seeing each other regularly. He'd make the drive from L.A. to my place in the valley, often after a long day at work. He scored major points with me for that because people avoid that 405 freeway commute at all costs. One Saturday morning, I promised him a pancake breakfast. I made the mistake of trying out a new healthy pancake mix on him. Normally, I would have taste tested a new recipe first. But no, I confidently encouraged him to dig in while my pancakes were still on the griddle cooking. By the time I joined him, he had eaten half of the pancakes. I took one bite and immediately grabbed my napkin to remove the repulsive morsel (OK, I spit it out). I looked at him and said, "Wait, do NOT take another bite!" I tasted his pancakes. I took his plate, threw the pancakes in the trash and said, "I can't believe you were eating that." "Well, you made it for me, I was getting through it," he replied sweetly and chuckled a little. They were supposed to be whole wheat, cinnamon, walnut pancakes but they tasted like YUCK! They were absolutely the worse thing I'd ever made; "Like ever!" (Using my valley girl voice). I redeemed myself over time with my usual good cooking, but he would get many laughs over the next few years at his re-telling of the pancake event.

Will and I shared a love for movies and music making it easy for us to bond over the latest flicks and his favorite, old school R&B. He had an extensive collection of music of all genres with an emphasis on R&B. As a result, my own collection has been enhanced with mix-tapes he made especially for me (actually CDs). An impromptu concert was bound to break out at any time and often did. It could be accompanied by a slightly off-key serenade from him. It was really cute.

When I introduced him to the family, he fit right in. That is after being teased about his name NOT being Paul or not being a musician. I just can't imagine why folks had stereotyped me as only dating musicians and men named Paul. I started feeling like Will was a keeper. The points were definitely adding up for him. We got along really well and enjoyed each other's company.

Will exhibited a hard-working get-it-done work ethic. I admired that quality in him. My attraction to him was strengthened by his field of business—home improvement. He was a contractor skilled in all aspects of the business. I would pitch in assisting him with the administrative tasks. My helping him was a double-edged sword. I could be a helpmate to him in one of my areas of strength, administration, but it also exposed the inner workings of how he handled life situations and business dealings.

This is where I found we differed greatly. I began to see the cracks in our relationship without the emotion of the health stuff I had been going through in the beginning. Looking back, I believe our relationship developed so quickly because of those health events. My practical mind reasoned if he could be by my side during such stressful times, we could face anything together. I let him in. The clock was ticking. We could make it work. Way deep down somewhere in my subconscious mind, a faint impression was saying, There will never be another Music Paul. It was a fleeting thought, but it had left a residue that told me to make this relationship work. I truly cared about this man. He could live with my stuff and I could live with his.

When Will asked me to marry him, he didn't make any romantic overtures, passionate prose on one knee, or even present me with a ring. It was more like an announcement to me that I was his woman. "Let's get married." Even so, I accepted his effortless proposal. I had been toying with the idea in my head; I wasn't getting any younger. The old lady with eight cats thing was in the back of my mind. With the benefit of hindsight, I should have been a lot more patient in the process. First, I should have required a proper proposal with a ring. Will bought me a temporary ring until he could afford something better, he said. We made plans to get married that summer sometime in between our birthdays.

But then… life happened. I'd see more cracks in us, but I'd be distracted again and again by the return of medical drama. I'd experience more medical procedures and surgeries, then heal, need another procedure, then more healing and rehab. It seemed to be a never-ending cycle of medical drama. We put off getting married and in the midst of it all, I changed my mind but kept that piece of information to myself. I didn't like what I was seeing in his behavior. I was also convinced that all of my medical drama was too taxing for him. I wouldn't blame him if it was because sometimes it was too taxing for me.

"We don't have to do this anymore."

At some point, I perceived things had changed. My intuition had been screaming, "Something is amiss! There's some extracurricular activities going on." We had moved to an open relationship without my knowledge or consent. Acting on my suspicion, I once told him, "We don't have to do this anymore. I know this is a lot for you to deal with." He adamantly declared that nothing was wrong, that we were good, and that he loved me.

We went on but his behavior was sometimes a little suspect. Eventually, social media would be the tattletale. I am not the type to nag and ask where have you been? Where are you going? I won't search your wallet or phone. My feelings are that you should trust the person you're with until they show you differently. So, I did try to give him the benefit of the doubt. That is, until I confirmed my suspicions completely by accident. There it was on a picture I had taken and posted of Will on my Facebook page. Right out in the open for anyone to see. The woman posted on the picture that, "She couldn't wait," and something about her "Big Daddy." It was then that I looked at his phone. He asked me why I was doing that. I told him about the FB post. He tried to deny it until I opened my FB page and showed it to him. "Oh shit!" was his response. "That's all you have to say for yourself? If that's what you want... fine!" Infidelity and outright lying were complete deal-breakers. We weren't even married yet. There was no screaming or hollering; no histrionics or drama. I imagine I could have been dramatic, crying, or anything else demonstrative and emotional. However, that wasn't me. It was just over. I didn't and still don't have energy to waste on nonsense. I didn't want to play anymore. I took my ball and went home.

Much later, I felt extremely grateful that I hadn't made the mistake of marrying him. We had some good times together; he just wasn't "the one." After the break-up, my medical situation became the targeted focus of my life; no time for taking any applications.

Sometimes it's just the right time for the wrong thing...
rather, the wrong person.

Taking Applications

Adventure Turned Journey

In the beginning, I dedicated this accounting to all of the people out there searching. Searching for what? Some might say for love, sex, companionship, money, power, fame, the perfect smile, body, tan, car, acceptance, etc. Doesn't really matter what it is that you think you're searching for. Material things won't satisfy that elusive thing you're seeking. I was looking for "the one"—my soul mate and life partner. In the process of my search and taking applications, I discovered me and so much more.

There is a yearning within each of us that longs for connection; a connection that surpasses any surface level, temporary, or outward pleasure. We can't always identify that internal yearning. It manifests as uniquely as we each individually have been created. The reality of the "it" is actually acceptance and unconditional love. It's that kind of love that is not expressed man to woman; woman to man; man to man; woman to woman; woman to child, animal, or anything else that we say, "I love" to or about.

The love we seek is the truest love of our Creator, agape love. We long for true connection. The cola company used to sell drinks with its jingle, "It's the real thing." However, love from God is the true real thing! He's the realest expression of love.

One of my favorite passages in the Word speaks on love. It reads: "Love is patient, love is kind. It does not envy, it does not boast, it is not proud. It does not dishonor others, it is not self-seeking, it is not easily angered, it keeps no record of wrongs. Love does not delight in evil but rejoices with the truth. It always protects, always trusts, always hopes, always perseveres. Love never fails."

Can you imagine having that kind of love in your life, whether for your mate, family, friends, neighbors, or fellow man? To strive for that type of love is a lofty ambition. We'd make our world a better place even if we only tried to live our lives practicing the first two: "Love is patient" and "Love is kind." To strive for the level of love written about in Corinthians is an on purpose exercise of choice. You have to move past the emotional feelings to choose to be patient and kind when normal reasoning and situations would have you be anything but patient and kind.

My viewpoints and paradigms change when I attempt to live out these principles. I cannot view things as God because I do not have the mind of God. We are all humanly flawed; however, reading and considering the details of the passage can give us a glimpse into the depth of God's love. Expressing love on the basis of unconditional intention is deep.

So often when watching a romantic chick flick, my heart would be full of longing for someone to love me as passionately as the scene playing out before me. Tears would spill out in spite of my stoic attitude. There would be such longing that my heart and bones would ache with the desire to have someone be so dramatically in love with me. To know that God loves me with a much deeper intensity than that is an awesome thing.

~ ~ ~

Frankly, I'm constantly learning how to do this thing called life… better.

~ ~ ~

This search transformed into an adventure. It was a series of sometimes funny, antidotal stories that have doubled as learning experiences lined with humor, sadness, immense joy, and a few good meals except for No Dinner Man and No Dinner Man Too. My growth through the process has been immeasurable. God has used my life's adventures to serve as cautionary, encouraging, and sometimes hilarious tales. Tales that had I not experienced firsthand would be difficult to believe.

Retrospectively reviewing many of the events opened my eyes. The journey and chronicling of it have been filled with self-discovery. I learned what I would and would not tolerate. I found a strength and sense of courage in the face of good and bad times. Frankly, I'm constantly learning how to do this thing called life… better. Battling with my own standards and those others have placed on me has influenced my actions on many occasions. Using wisdom and patience to listen to the inner voice trying to lead me correctly has been a product of the learning process.

My hope in sharing some of my experiences along the way is to spur laughter, thoughtfulness, on purpose intentions, healing, and inspiration to trust in God. I have had a certain trust in God since I was a young girl. That trust has matured as I have aged and grown closer to Him. He has been with me since the day I accepted Him. No matter what adventures come my way, God is with me and He has already blessed me with His ultimate love…

I found The One!

Taking Applications

Grateful

Thank you

God, for always having my back, front, beginning, middle, and everything else... especially when I haven't had a clue what I was doing, which is more often than I can know, fathom, or express.

Thank you to every early listener of the adventures I relayed; for your encouragement to write and then finish the manuscript after taking an extended hiatus from writing. Thank you for your love, support and prayers. To all of my honest, dedicated beta readers, I appreciate every comment, critique and encouragement.

Special thanks to:

Ruby Holland, my wonderful friend and sister in Christ. Your support, encouragement and 1st draft edits were invaluable.

Ty Scott King, you made the editing process a joy! Love U!

PeQue Brown, My amazing brother, friend and artist. This book would not have been possible without your love, support and amazing artistic contributions. Your illustrations bought my visions to life!

Taking Applications

love love love love... (background repeated)

Amore

J'adore

Preeti

mahabba

Dragoste

Láska

giniguma

Kohania

Love

Ciuta

Prema

Mahal

L'amore

Pyaar

Rak

Miłość

Sneham

Влюблённость

Agapee

Amore

Sinta

Inirog

Lubov

Liefde

Rakastaa

Taking Applications

www.ingramcontent.com/pod-product-compliance
Lightning Source LLC
Chambersburg PA
CBHW060336030426
42336CB00011B/1375